PAPERWEIGHTS

OF THE WORLD

PAPERWEIGHTS

OF THE WORLD

by Monika Flemming
and
Peter Pommerencke

WITH PRICE GUIDE

Schiffer Publishing Ltd

77 Lower Valley Road, Atglen, PA 19310

Back Cover Picture

Selkirk Glass, Scotland
"Sea Mist", modern design, 1991, 500 produced. Diameter 8.5 cm. Signature hand-engraved
on the base: Selkirk Glass Scotland, "Sea Mist", serial number, quantity made and year.
    $120

Frontispiece
"La Marquise de Pompadour". Saint-Louis, France, 1845, replica 1992. Height 320 mm.

Copyright © 1993 by
Schiffer Publishing Ltd.

Library of Congress Catalog Number: 93-87045
All rights reserved. No part of this work may be reproduced or used in any forms or by any means – graphic,
electronic or mechanical, including photocopying or
information storage and retrieval systems – without
written permission from the copyright holder.

Translated by Dr. Edward Force,
Central Connecticut State University.

Printed in the United States of America.
ISBN: 0-88740-592-4

We are interested in hearing from authors
with book ideas on related topics.

Published by Schiffer Publishing Ltd.
77 Lower Valley Road
Atglen, PA 19310
Please write for a free catalog.
This book may be purchased from the publisher.
Please include $2.95 postage.
Try your bookstore first.

Contents

INTRODUCTION
Paperweights, today as 150 years ago, a lovely anachronism   7

History and Development of the Paperweight
Glassmaking in Ancient Egypt and the Near East   9
The Importance of Rome in Glass Distribution   10
The Importance of Venice   10
The First Paperweights   11
Pietro Bigaglia, the Murano Glassmaker   11
Venice Sets the Course of Glass in Europe   13
Paperweights via Bohemia, France and Britain   13
The Concept of "Paperweight"   15

Paperweight Production
Glass—the Material and its Processing   17
The Technique of Melting Glass   18
The California Paperweight Technique   21

Paperweight Makers
Bohemia and Silesia (circa 1840-1930)   22
Bohemian "Letter-weights"
     Pause Work from Bohemia, Silesia, Thuringia,
     Saxony and Bavaria (1890-1945, 1960 to date)   23
Murano—Venice (circa 1840 to date)   25
Baccarat (1764 to date)   26
Clichy (1837-1870)   27
Saint-Louis (1767 to date)   29
Pantin (1850-1890)   29
Whitefriars (1680-1980)   30
Bacchus (circa 1850)   32
Perthshire (1968 to date)   32
Paul Ysart   33
Caithness Glass (1969 to date)   34
Selkirk Glass (1977 to date)   34
"J" Glass by John Deacons (1979-1983, 1987 to date)   35
China (1930 to date)   35
America (1850-1885)   36

The Glass Studios
Studio-Glass Paperweights 38
Correia Art Glass 39
Abelman Art Glass 39
Lotton Art Glass 40
Lundberg Studio Glass 40
Orient & Flume Art Glass 41
Parabelle Glass 42
Josh Simpson Glass 42

Independent Artists
Lampwork Paperweights 43
Roland ("Rick") Ayotte 44
Ray and Bob Banford 45
Christopher ("Chris") Buzzini 46
Jim Donofrio 46
John Gooderham 47
Randall ("Randy") Grubb 47
Harold Hacker, Robert and Ronald Hansen 48
Charles Kaziun 48
James and Nontas Kontes 49
Dominick Labino 49
Johne Parsley and Gordon Smith 49
Ken Rosenfeld 50
Barry Sautner 51
Paul Joseph Stankard 51
Delmo and Debbie Tarsitano 52
Victor Trabucco and Sons Jon and David Trabucco 52
Mayauel Ward 53
Francis Whittemore 53

Hints for Collectors 54

The Care of Paperweights 56

Glossary 57

Museums with Paperweight Collections 60

Photo Credits 61

Bibliography 62

ILLUSTRATIONS

Paperweight Illustrations 63
About the Illustrations and the Price Guide

INDEX OF MAKERS 167

Introduction

Paperweights—today as 150 years ago, a lovely anachronism

Caution: the passion for collecting beautiful paperweights is contagious! What is the secret of this boom in collecting paperweights that has thrived for more than thirty years? The paperweight is a microcosm in the hands of those people who have selected them and enjoy them. A paperweight, or "letter weight", was already an anachronism just a few years after it was created in the middle of the past century, and it certainly is one today.

Never has more been written than today. Never before have more letters been sent—millions upon millions every day. But the overwhelming majority of these letters are computer-generated business letters. Letters that never require a paper-weight and scarcely a file. Decorated little private writing-desks to hold them, such as were found in every middle-class house at one time, have not existed for over a century. Today's paper lies in stacks on office desks. It runs just as smoothly through the shredder and piles up to form mountains at recycling depots. Who needs genuine letter weights today, to say nothing of genuine paperweights?

And yet, genuine paperweights have their best chances in this time of modern objectivity. Just as there will always be people who prefer hand-sewn shoes, or those who know and love real handmade carpets. The genuine article, of high quality, will always be around. Those who have the resources to surround themselves with beautiful, valuable things may well turn to paperweights as fascinating collectors' items.

Both authors have collected paperweights for some twenty years, and since 1976 they have run Germany's first and, for some time, only paperweight dealership. Their worldwide contact with all the manufacturers and artists and their intensive exchange of experience with fellow dealers on an international level have made them experts whose advice is valued by beginner and connoisseur alike.

The tireless involvement of both authors with these exquisite objects of art has also predestined them to active collaboration in the Paperweight Club of Germany in Munich. They have mastered their subject; in this book you will find a thorough answer to every question. It offers advice, pictures, a price guide and a great deal of background information on an exciting area of collecting.

The famous French writer, Colette, owned a choice collection of paperweights. Her daughter, Mme. Colette de Jouvenel, once wrote in a letter to the director of the time-honored Cristallerie de Saint-Louis, Gerard Ingold, himself a devoted paperweight collector and connoisseur, the striking sentence:
"Whoever has the ability to make emeralds and sapphires arise out of glass, captures the tones of color that only occur fleetingly in nature, the real and unreal shapes and colors, in an object no bigger than the palm of your hand—he may be only a modest magician, but he is a magician all the same."

History and Development of the Paperweight

Glassmaking in Ancient Egypt and the Near East

The art of making glass is more than five thousand years old. More than 3000 years before Christ, artisans in Egypt or parts of western Asia (Syria, Mesopotamia) found the traces of glass, melted by chance, probably at the edges of fire sites in the quartz sand of the desert. Perhaps it was only a suggestion of glazing over the glowing stones on the hearth at first.

Though man had long since used natural glass—the volcanic rock obsidian—to make tools and weapons, the history of artificial glass probably began in the Nile Valley of old Egypt or on the banks of the Tigris and Euphrates in Mesopotamia. Referring to glass as the oldest "artificial material" in the world surely does not seem completely illogical, though it is not correct in a scientific sense.

Man's inventiveness in working with this new material developed quickly. Soon costly jewelry was created, at first only in massive form. Glazes for earthen and glass vessels were developed later, at first only in small quantities, but development proceeded quickly.

Since the glassmaker's blowpipe had not yet been invented and the people of Egypt and the Near East had no heat-tolerant material to use for crucibles in which glass could be melted, any and all glass objects had to be made by means of sintering. In this form of melting in which quantities of glass were baked, the glass, only poorly melted because the heat was far from sufficient, was taken in a barely liquid form and shaped around a clay or sand form or pressed into a curved vessel mold. The similarity to ceramics—a technique which man already knew—is great.

Thus long before the blowpipe was invented, many centuries before Christ, the first ornaments, bowls and bottles were made by this sintering technique of pressing and shaping semi-liquid glass around forms. After the glass had cooled, the forms were carefully and laboriously removed from the vessels.

Bright colored glass was surely created at first only by still-unknown chemical impurities in the glass mixtures. It is possible that man had already tried using various quartz sands, mixed them together, and later combined them with other minerals to attain a variety of colors. With that, the artisans of the Nile, Euphrates and Tigris were able to melt colored glass and apply it laboriously to the outside of the vessels for more than three thousand years. By applying colored glass plates side by side, after making them individually by pressing and squeezing, they could produce amulets and colorful mosaic vessels.

The oldest known shards and fragments of glass vessels have been dated by scientists as coming from the 15th and 16th centuries before Christ. They came from western Asia, the northernmost part of present-day Iraq (Niniveh, northern Mesopotamia), and thus rank as somewhat older than the many early discoveries from Egypt.

Only some two to three thousand years later, in late-Renaissance (mid-sixteenth century) Venice, would the name Millefiori be invented for a portion of this mosaic glass.

The Importance of Rome in Glass Distribution

After the fall of the Greek empire, Rome expanded its sphere of influence in the Mediterranean area farther, via North Africa in the direction of Asia Minor. Glass vessels from occupied Egypt and from Syria were imported, and the technique of glass production reached Rome and later Venice.

The most important glassmaker's tool—the blowpipe, a hollow, bored-out iron rod—was invented in Syria around 100 B.C. The development of better crucible material made it possible to melt glass to a more liquid state. Only then was it possible to make hollow glass.

The Romans' mighty campaigns over the Alps and far into the Rhineland, to Gaul, Spain and even Britain, along with long-standing garrisoning and settling of those lands, soon spread glass production over almost all of Europe. The art of glass-blowing, already very highly developed in all of southern and central Europe at the time of the Roman Empire, is proved by the discovery of impressive glass objects that we can see today in almost all of our major museums. Surely one of the best examples is the Roman-Germanic Museum in Cologne on the Rhine.

From the fifth to the middle of the fifteenth century A.D., there is almost nothing to report on the development of man-made glass in Europe. The advent of this "glassless" era accompanied the decline of the highly developed and influential Roman Empire.

Roman mosaic bowl. First century A.D. Diameter 155 mm. Victoria and Albert Museum, London.

The Importance of Venice

Only as of the mid-fifteenth century did a tendency toward producing more complex, more beautiful artistically formed glass slowly begin to occur. In the sixteenth and seventeenth centuries, the glass art of Venice led the way to new development. The renowned, filigree glass first appeared among Venetian glassware. The technique of making millefiori glass, forgotten since ancient days, appeared again.

In the mid-seventeenth and eighteenth centuries, glassworks all over Europe and special crystal works in France had regal purposes. This was assuredly so in France, to be sure of meeting the nobility's need for candelabra and costly table crystal.

Besides the primary need for glass to make bottles, jugs, bowls, cups and, most of all, drinking glasses of almost every type, a new use for man-made glass appeared toward the end of the eighteenth century. It was used more and more often to make completely secular decorative and utilitarian objects, which were not always made of hollow glass.

Diatret glass. Rome, 100-200 A.D.

Old glass oven from the 17th century.

The First Paperweights

Slowly at first and then more and more quickly, a very expensive product, paper, spread throughout Europe, having also made its way from Asia via Egypt and North Africa to Italy. This followed a similar course to that of glass, but occurred 1500 years later.

With the greater spread of paper, which was used not only for book production, reading and writing became more widespread. At first, royal messengers carried documents and other official messages from court to court; the house of Taxis, later Thurn und Taxis, was charged with the great organizational effort that it required. Over the centuries, the European postal system developed. A regular exchange of mail, primarily of letters, was soon possible for everyone. The first official postage stamps in the present-day sense to be issued by a postal system appeared in Britain in 1840. Other countries, such as Switzerland, France and Belgium, quickly followed this example; Bavaria did so only in 1849, Prussia and Saxony one year later.

Only in the middle of the nineteenth century did the railroad link several important places in Europe. Thus letter writing ranked second only to laborious travel in mail coaches as the most important form of communication.

Letters piled up in the desk at home or in the office. The possibility of a sudden breeze or draft was always present; in less than a second it could ruin the finest organization of a stack of papers. Paperweights (letter weights) were quite necessary at that time, if one wanted to maintain the order of their papers and letters.

In the eighteenth century, such weights made of wood, precious and other metals, rock such as marble, leather bags filled with sand, or hemispheres of glass or ceramic were already in existence. For years before then, these various types of weights had also been used to hold rolled documents open, which had existed for centuries in the form of parchment rolls.

Pietor Bigaglia, the Murano Glassmaker

For the glass-blowers of the early nineteenth century it was important to produce weights according to supply and demand. They could be made quickly and simply. The first blob of glass that the glass-blower takes from the melting pot with his blowpipe is always and immediately as round as a ball, with scarcely any further processing needed. If the glass-blower then lets this semi-liquid blob of glass drip on bits of colored glass or colored glass canes, and then "presses in" inclusions into the once again liquid glass and shapes it, the paperweight is already half-created.

It must have happened just this way in the glassworks of Pietro Bigaglia at Murano some 150 years ago. By evening there were always many bits of colored glass on the glass-makers' and glass-blowers' workbenches. They would include millefiori and filigree rods, aventurine glass and other colored glass, left over as the garbage of the day's production (cups, bottles, flagons, bowls, all kinds of writing-desk utensils such as penholder bowls, ink bottles, ink rollers, as well as glass handles and vases).

The glassworks were still experimenting with colored glass to the early and mid-nineteenth century. Previously, for thousands of years and into the seventeenth century, glass was tinted more or less accidentally by the impurities in the material. Cleansing processes could not always be carried out under chemically reliable control, and these small impurities in the mixture produced differing shades of color. Sometimes the glass darkened later by photochemical processes in the chemically impure glass. The recipes used to color Roman glass had been forgotten.

In this respect, it should be kept in mind that in the service of the Great Elector of Brandenburg, Johann Kunckel worked hard to carry out his experiments and produce gold ruby glass at Potsdam a century and a half earlier. The processes of making gold ruby glass and other colored glass, though, were already known in Italy at the end of the sixteenth or the beginning of the seventeenth century, which was some seventy years before Kunckel's experiments.

From about 1840 on, all the glassworks had colored glass available or could produce it easily. The chemistry used in the technology of glassmaking also made more and more progress. The coloring and melting of colored glass, especially metallic salts and metallic oxides, became simpler all the time, involving the controlled use of chemicals available from large-scale technical firms. An ever-greater variety could be had, and they could be used more easily by anyone.

The easy, uncomplicated production and availability of colored glass at this time made work simple for the glass-blowers. The shaping and drawing of glass rods and canes had been invented anew in Venice two hundred years before (see also "Paperweight Production").

Pietro Bigaglia probably was the first glass-blower whose "colorful glass balls" attracted a great deal of attention from the public. Venice and Lombardy still belonged at that time to the polyglot state of the Imperial and Royal Habsburg Empire, centered in Vienna. This allowed direct connections with the Austrian-Bohemian glassworks, which were competing against others, especially those in Britain and France, with their brilliant lead crystal at that time. Bigaglia exhibited his paperweights at the Vienna Industrial Exposition in 1845, and they attracted attention. In the very same year, the renowned French crystal works at Saint-Louis produced their first examples.

Pietro Bigaglia paperweight,
1845.

Venice Sets the Course of Glass in Europe

The maritime republic of Venice, a great commercial power, was known into the eighteenth century as the world's leading producer of glass.

It is often thought that the banishing of the glassworks from the islands of Venice to the small nearby island of Murano at the end of the thirteenth century was done to protect their secrets. This probably is not completely correct, since the great majority of the many hundred glass workers could not live on the small island permanently.

Under threat of the most severe punishment, the Venetian glass-blowers were forbidden for centuries to talk about glass production or to leave the republic. The founding of many glassworks far away from Venice, though, involved Venetian glassmakers.

Glass production outside Venice was based on that successful example. Until into the eighteenth century, production almost everywhere was carried out "à la façon de Venise."

Like the first steps in the discovery of man-made glass in North Africa or the Near East, the first steps in the development of the paperweight, primarily the millefiori paperweight, are largely unknown.

This much is sure: Venice, Bohemia, Austrian and Prussian Silesia and French Alsace-Lorraine were areas in which glassmaking played a major role; German was spoken and commercial contact with each other was maintained. Thus language was not a barrier. Not only carpenters made long trips in their business lives, but so did the glassmakers and glass dealers who traveled far in Europe.

Much must have happened simultaneously and without much planning when the first paperweights came into being in the 1840s. Everyone knew what kind of work his colleagues were doing, and much experimentation was done in this field. No other handicraft was better suited to experimentation, for the raw material of glass is relatively cheap, becoming expensive only through the costs of production and damaged goods. Also, it can be worked quickly. The first results of experimentation can be seen within a few minutes as it is being worked, and on the next day in the cooled object.

Thus it is imaginable, as so often in discoveries and inventions, that chance must have played a major role in the creation of the paperweight.

Paperweights via Bohemia, France and Britain

Millefiori glass was known in Bohemia just as it was in Murano. Even in the times before 1840, such ornamentation was used in and on Bohemian glassware. Perhaps they were already experimenting with millefiori glass at Baccarat and Saint-Louis in France before the news of millefiori glass was heard from the industrial exposition at Vienna in 1845. Many decades before that, good results had been achieved with the "pastelike" production of glass medallions, which the Englishman Apsley Pellat, Jr. had begun, perfected, and described in books between 1820 and 1840. So experimentation went on everywhere at the same time.

The first Saint-Louis paperweight also dates from the year of 1845. Baccarat followed in 1846, as did the Clichy works in Paris. In 1848 Bacchus of Birmingham displayed its products, undated millefiori paperweights, at industrial expositions. Clichy displayed paperweights at the significant first World Exposition at the Crystal Palace in London in 1851.

Who would have thought that these colorful little balls of glass would ever take on so much interest among a large international community of collectors?

Had they perhaps been described earlier only as "letter weights"? In Germany, to be sure, they were called "Briefbeschwerer" (letter weights) from the start, but they scarcely existed there. In Bohemia and Silesia too, they had not been produced in significant quantities. They did not appear in the glassworks catalogs. From their rare appearances on the market in Germany, Austria and Czechoslovakia today it can be concluded that they were nothing more than individual pieces or experiments that were made by only a few glass-blowers in only a few glassworks.

It is estimated today that in the three significant French crystal works of Saint-Louis, Baccarat, and Clichy, production added up to only 25,000 examples at most. This covers the entire production period from 1846 to about 1860! This cannot have been a great commercial success. Other sources, especially those based on American viewpoints, cite much lower figures.

No information on possible production at Murano can be found. Only two or three dozen of these "fermacarte" are known today. But letter weights of every other kind exist in great quantities, for they were as necessary in their day as penholders, ink bottles and blotting paper.

It should be emphasized here and kept in mind that this small and short-term production of the French glassworks probably was not terribly style-oriented from the beginning and did not exactly correspond to the tastes of the upper classes. The greater part of the population could not afford these products, or any other glassware from the fine French crystal works, in any case.

Since letter weights were in almost every household and also made of other materials, how else can it be explained that the three largest and best-known French crystal works could not succeed in building the trade in letter weights into a greater success? It must also be noted that the crystal works of Saint-Louis and Baccarat in France were much larger and more important at that time than they are today.

Baccarat, dated 1847. "Macédoine"—colorful millefiori cane sections arranged in a web pattern. Diameter 5.7 cm. $610

It is thought that this paperweight was made circa 1930 (so-called Dupont paperweight) and thus has a false date cane. The individual millefiori sections that are scattered on the back of the model are very interesting, as they are thoroughly identical to those in dated close millefiori paperweights by Baccarat, made in 1848.

The uneasy times in particular ruled out great success. It should be kept in mind that the relatively long and stable era of absolutism was followed by Napoleon I with his military campaigns in half of Europe and his ultimate downfall at Waterloo. War debts, citizen kings and a deep economic depression characterized the restoration era, which had as its outcome the next revolution in February of 1848. Grinding poverty prevailed among the people, along with the start of industrialization and mass production.

This was all linked to a great decline in all handicraft production, including that of artistic, individually produced glass. Who could have any interest then in such luxuries? This decline was interrupted only briefly from the turn of the century to World War I by the era of Jugendstil and Art Nouveau, with products from France, especially Nancy, Austrian Bohemia, and Alsace-Lorraine which was then part of Imperial Germany.

Thus it was left for our generation to discover and appreciate these beautiful works of art. Like many things from the days when pure handicraft prevailed, paperweights were made with great love for details and great care. Even if we do not definitely know where and by whom they were first made, and even if we sometimes have trouble identifying and classifying them and can only guess why their production was halted after a short time, we can be content that at least the way they were made can be reconstructed in our own times.

The Concept of "Paperweight"

In the nineteenth century genuine, practical (and impractical) paperweights of a great variety of materials reached their pinnacle. One will find that the term used was almost always "letter-weights." Logically, weights to hold down letters are "letter-weights." But since the French were leaders from the start in the realm of the "colorful glass balls," rather than that of actual letter weights, we must look into the French language to find an explanation. Here, parallel to the term "boule de sulfure," the term "presse-papier" soon came into being. The term "lettre-presse" or "presse-lettre" did not catch on.

It was inevitable that, with the spread of this very special French "letter-weight", the "paper presser", into Britain and America, only the corresponding English expression became popular. But since hardly anyone still used these colorful spheres to hold down letters and since they were not ideal for the purpose and no longer modern, it was of no importance whether they were still called "letter-weights" or "paperweights" in English. For every English-speaking person, "paperweight" was the literal and correct translation of the French term "presse-papier". Thus the term "paperweight", via the English language, spread very quickly throughout the world.

Since the utensil originally called the "letter-weight" has disappeared almost completely from our present-day daily life, so too has the word, first from everyday use and then from dictionaries. Genuine, truly useful letter-weights have been unknown to most people for many years.

Meanwhile, countless individuals have come to collect these colorful glass balls that, to be sure, are at home mostly in the USA. Books about paperweights have been written almost exclusively in the English language. Since the German language, because of its strong political and economic ties with the West, happily absorbs all sorts of Americanisms, it is no surprise that the word "paperweight" was picked up so quickly.

The paperweight collectors in Germany know that the word *Briefbeschwerer* in addition to its original application to actual letter-weights, can also apply to glass objects of varying shapes and colors. Paperweight and Briefbeschwerer often overlap. Often it is only a personal, subjective inclination to a paperweight that makes them choose one word or the other. But a "paperweight" is limited to a "Briefbeschwerer" made of glass or crystal around the middle of the nineteenth century, and mostly made at the well-known glassworks of France, Britain, America, Venice or Bohemia. Or alternatively, it applies not to a piece of work from those particular glassworks or to a genuine antique, but to present-day objects made in the old style usually at the traditional glassworks, or by laborious methods by individual artists in glass studios. Good examples of this are Saint-Louis and Baccarat in France; and Paul Stankard, Rick Ayotte and the Lundberg Studios group, all in the USA.

A completely new type of noteworthy and desirable paperweights are those that have reached Germany since the seventies, at first from Caithness Glass and since 1978 also from Selkirk Glass. Completely new glass techniques and technologies have made it possible for creative young glass-blowers to conjure up a futuristic world or enchanting scenes, made of countless air bubbles, swirls of color, veils, reflections and various colors and shapes, all in the small world of the paperweight.

There will always be borderline cases that are "only" Briefbeschwerer or "just" paperweights, and every paperweight collector knows this. In the end, the collector himself decides on the quality of his collection. Everything is relative, and subjectivity plays an important role. It remains a very personal area of collecting that can never be completed and chronicled without a gap. The concept of the paperweight has found a home not only in Germany and the English-speaking countries. In France, Italy and Spain too, the collectors speak of paperweights, although there too, as in Germany, the old names for the "Briefbeschwerer" are still known. They are:

English: letter-weight (old), paperweight
French: presse-papier
Italian: fermacarta
Spanish: pisapapeles

Paperweight Production

Glass—the material and its processing

The very stuff of which collectors' dreams are made, the clear and colored glass or crystal for paperweights, has an indescribable fascination. Glass is made of a simple mix of just a few inorganic raw materials: silica compounds in the form of sand, siliceous earth or quartz, are melted with the help of potash or soda and various other raw materials, gray and red chemicals.

According to the glassworks' recipe, the ingredients are mixed in only slightly changed quantity proportions, with the proportion of fine white glassmakers' sand always in the great majority of 60-80%. The mixture, with small amounts of several special chemicals and larger quantities of glass fragments added, is melted in small crucible, large vessel, tub or modern kilns at temperatures of 1400 to 1500 degrees. In comparison, the melting point of iron is also a little over 1500 degrees.

After the passage of melting and clarifying times of varying lengths (up to twenty hours, depending on the type of kiln, the raw materials and chemicals), the glowing, semi-liquid, slightly cooled, glass melt can be shaped and worked at a temperature of about 100 degrees. With the simplest glassmaking tools, scarcely changed in 2000 years—iron rods, blowpipes and pontils, as well as several wet wooden devices—a capable glass-blower can now form and shape the hot, flowing glass as he wishes and envisions. He is scarcely given any limits in formation.

The glass scarcely sets any limits for a good glass artist. By constant, repeated heating the artist can keep the glass just as liquid or elastic as he needs in order to shape it. Here the layman finds the explanation of a very fascinating mystery of glass: Just barely liquid and just solidified are very close. The two conditions are separated only by a small temperature difference of a few degrees—almost without transition. This special quality of glass is what gives the glass artist the chance to realize all of his creativity in works of art.

How many of today's glass artists utilize this unique physical quality of glass in creating their works? Only a few. But it is almost always the paperweight artists who, by fully exhausting all the fantastic qualities of glass, form their works just as they conceive them as artists. Not the other way around, with the glass determining how well the "work of art" succeeds. That would scarcely be art, but rather chance.

In the sovereign control of the balance between the slow flow of the glass in the shaping process and the slow cooling on the one hand and the quickly attained hardness on the other, the true master proves himself. Just as he controls clear, colorless glass in the work process, he can also melt and model bright, colorful glass, using one color, mixing or layering more.

Similarly to sculptors and painters, these artists use their ability, their tools and materials to give free expression to their feelings.

Above: Simple tools of the glassmaker. Center: Shaping glass in a model. Below: Copper-wheel engraving.

Shaping the first blob of glass with wet paper.

17

The technique of melting glass

The traditional technique, known for almost three thousand years, allows the glass-blower and glass artist to take relatively thin-flowing glass out of the melting kiln regularly. This glowing glass can be worked at once, and set in and enclose in it the previously modeled inclusions such as flowers, animals and millefiori sections.

The production of paperweights in the traditional manner could be done only in glassworks or crystal works until about thirty years ago. The best examples of this are Murano, Baccarat and Saint-Louis. Since the beginning of the sixties, though, smaller kilns known as studio kilns have been developed and now make it possible for smaller groups of artists in glass studios to work with oven glass. To produce the traditional, classic millefiori paperweights, one needs first the millefiori canes, which are sawed, cut, hacked or broken into small pieces (candy). The desired quality of the finished paperweight determines the complexity and care involved in carrying out the individual work processes.

But before the millefiori canes can be cut up, they have to be produced in many laborious individual steps of tedious handwork.

In a large glassworks or crystal works, not only clear glass or crystal but also various colored glass is melted in smaller melting kilns. The colored glass is needed for colored drinking glasses which often are provided later with a richly cut decoration that goes through the colored overlay.

Millefiori from Murano, Italy.

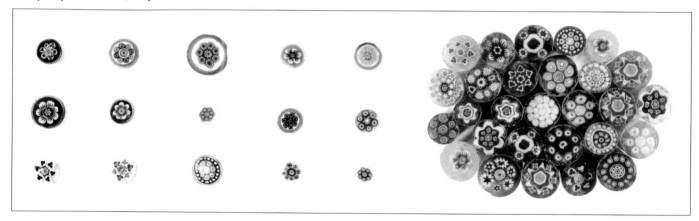

Filigree glass from Murano, Italy. Paperweight with porcelain medallions, from Saint-Louis, France, 1967.

These various colored glasses are the prerequisite for the colorful millefiori canes. Drops of glass weighing some two to three kilograms are cast in iron molds (models). These heavy iron molds show the outlines of the various stars, many other graphic and geometric designs, and many silhouettes of animals and fabulous creatures. The thick glass drop thus preformed and squeezed into these outlines is removed after being dipped briefly into the iron mold and then covered (overlaid) with the next layer of clear or colored glass, in order to keep it in shape. Through repeated shaping, also in other outline molds, and renewed overlaying with other colored glass, the glassblower can give free rein to his desires. This is the basis of the first millefiori canes. Seizing them at both ends with the glassmaker's pontils (heavy massive iron rods with covered ends), two glassmakers now begin to stretch these thick and heavy "glass drops" into thin canes, one or two centimeters thick and many meters long. The canes for the fine filigree canes must be turned constantly during stretching. The drawn-out glass cane, which cools very quickly, is laid on the floor and immediately broken into short, handy pieces.

Filigree glass from Murano, Italy.

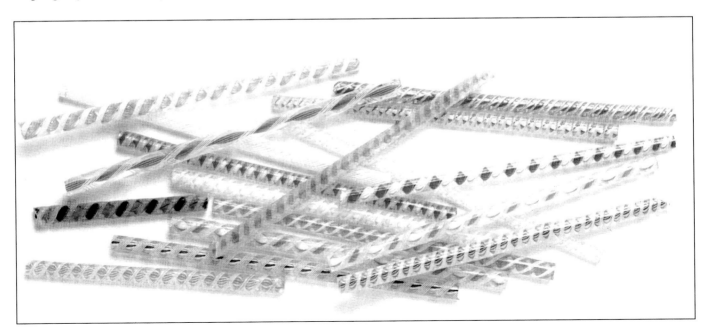

Often taking all day, the wearisome work of drawing out the canes determines the quality and price of the finished paperweight. The more times the individual work processes are repeated, the more complex is every single cane in its cross-section picture. A single cane can show a simple star or circle in an inexpensive paperweight, but in an expensive one it is made up of many dozens of individual motifs (multiple, complex millefiori canes).

With these small millefiori canes, the various pictorial motifs are laid in a round, massive iron form by hand and with forceps, a job that takes hours. Only when the motif has been finished does it go back to the glassworks in the iron form, to be melted carefully into the clear crystal-glass sphere. The slightest error of the glass-blower, the wrong temperature, too-short or too-long molding of the hot glass, air bubbles or impurities in the glass, etc., can lead to the ruin of the paperweight—after hours or even days of preliminary work have been put into it. The magnifying power of the surrounding glass brings out every unevenness, making it stand forth clearly.

Millefiori paperweight: Materials and the finished work of art.

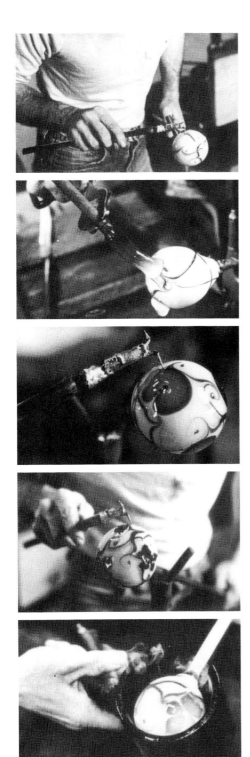

California paperweight technique: "painting" in glowing glass at Orient & Flume.

The California Paperweight Technique

Only since about twenty years ago have the paperweight artists in the glass studios of California developed, refined and made controllable a completely new glass-painting technique for producing paperweights of hot glass. Although it is known as a completely new technique of paperweight production, this idea of "painting" in and on glowing glass has been around for some time.

Since the turn of the century, work has been done at various glassworks (such as Tiffany in the USA and Loetz in Bohemia, Austria), in which the glass-blowers "painted" various "colors" (colored glass) onto the surface of the still semi-liquid glass by using a pointed iron spike to push and pull the fibers of colored glass. The process is very simple but very effective and striking. Then a thin film of metal-salt chemical was sprayed onto the glowing glass, achieving an iridescent, almost metallic effect that made the glass look superb.

Today these products of Loetz and Tiffany have become very popular and thus very expensive. Beware of fakes. The paperweight collector should know: The age and originality of the glass are hard to see and scarcely to be proved. Complex shapes that cannot, or cannot easily, be copied occur only rarely in old vases.

Paperweight collectors have it a little easier. Actual falsifications of genuine old, and thus very valuable, paperweights have not appeared to date. All the same, be careful: imitation, falsification and other types of "unnoticeables" occur very often in paperweights.

The painting technique used on the Loetz and Tiffany vases was developed extensively by a few young glass artists from California, at first and mainly at Orient & Flume and Lundberg, later Correia and Abelman. Along with relatively simple vases and world-famous tulip-shaped lamp chimneys made by the same technique as by Loetz and Tiffany around the turn of the century, such complex works of art are being made today that one cannot help but wonder whether it was glass artists who created them. Painters and sculptors in one person seem to have created these works of art in and of glass. But they are actually "only" glass artists. With endless patience, they paint and shape the motifs, colors and shapes on the fluid glass object in superb, generally naturalistic portrayals. Again and again they apply and melt new and different colored glass, either by themselves or with the help of a colleague, and then paint and shape them delicately on the glowing glass with relatively crude instruments. Meanwhile the objects must be reheated again and again. Many layers of overlay are applied in laborious, seemingly endless work. Again and again the process of painting is demonstrated on these new surfaces of glass.

In the same manner, these artists form their paperweights, and this level of perfection and quality has been achieved only in California to date. Since paperweights are not hollow, there is naturally no need to blow them. Only the modern kiln and burner technology on the one hand, and the youthful, perfectionist spirit of the American glass artists on the other, have made it possible to create these unique Californian works of glass art.

Paperweight Makers

Bohemia and Silesia (circa 1840 and 1880-1930)

Names such as Josephinenhütte, Riedelsche Hütte, Antoniwald or Harrachsche Hütte are those of glassworks in the present-day three-nation area of Germany, Poland and the Czech Republic. This district was formerly ruled by Austria, later by Prussia. The glassworks named above as examples were known to only a few interested glass specialists until a few years ago. Called forth by the ever-growing interest in paperweights in recent years, they turn up today in isolated but striking millefiori paperweights that cannot simply be attributed to the three renowned French crystal works of Saint-Louis, Baccarat and Clichy.

There are always such pieces that seem very similar to those of the three well-known French crystal works, but on closer observation the collector notices at first small, then significant differences. These can be: The color of the glass tends toward gray, sometimes to yellowish, unlike the French, which always glows bright white, or often blue-white. The pieces from Bohemia or Silesia are made of a glass that has been typical of this region for centuries. It has no lead added to it at all. Thus it is a relatively hard glass that is little suited to cutting and polishing. It is not lead-crystal glass. The French began to make lead-crystal glass at Saint-Louis in 1871, about a hundred years after its first discovery (in Britain, at the end of the 17th century). These lesser-known paperweights, perhaps from those Bohemian and Silesian glassworks, are the same size as the French or British ones but considerably lighter in weight. Millefiori canes that are fully identical to the comparable French types are never found.

Every kind of millefiori pattern that occurs in the French paperweights is also known in the Bohemian and Silesian paperweights. Crown weights were also made. Millefiori on a filigree background is relatively common. Swirls with individual millefiori canes, overlays with windows and other complicated cuts, and even paperweights painted on the surface of the glass are known. In the richness of variety there are scarcely any differences from the French paperweights. Silhouette canes with animals, butterflies, dancing figures, devils, eagles and (Austrian) double eagles also turn up again and again. The number of geometrical motifs in the canes is similar to those of the French paperweights.

The number of glassworks in Bohemia and Silesia was still very great around 1840. In spite of that, such paperweights as were produced in great, noteworthy numbers in France turn up very rarely. Although more paperweights from the last century can be traced to Bohemia or Silesia than was the case not too many years ago, the total number is still very small. They are more numerous than those from Murano. In Bohemia and Silesia in that part of the past century there were considerably more glassworks. Here production had not been expanded as much as in France. They simply did not have as extensive markets as did France with its capital of Paris.

Considerably lower production in these old glassmaking regions of Austria and Prussia would explain the well-known shortage of paperweights in German-speaking countries.

Peaceful relations between Germany and France, and corresponding trade relations, were not assured at that time. It can be assumed that Bohemian and Silesian paperweights hardly ever reached France, nor did French products reach Germany.

Old Bohemian and Silesian millefiori paperweights made in the nineteenth century are presently increasing greatly in value. They are quite pleasant works, and then too, the numbers of paperweight collectors in Germany and Austria are increasing constantly. Such paperweights simply cannot be reproduced any more. From the end of the nineteenth century to the twenties and thirties of this century it was very common for the glass blowers to produce so-called "friggers" during their breaks or at the end of the day. These paperweights were always given away by the glass-blowers. Sometimes names, places and/or dates on the paperweights refer to the recipients and the occasion. The values of these letter-weights depend very much on their origin and, above all, their beauty. Prices range from $50 to $500.

Bohemian "Letter-Weights"—Friggers from Bohemia, Silesia, Saxony, Thuringia and Bavaria (1880-1945, 1960 to date)

In the "land of a thousand glassworks", in the neighboring areas of Silesia, northern Bohemia, the Sudetenland, the Erzgebirge, Thuringia, the Fichtelgebirge, the Böhmerwald and Bayerwald, friggers were always made by the glass-blowers and accepted by the works management.

In the beginning, and for centuries, hard work and short breaks made these pieces quite rare, but as of about the turn of the century the prescribed work hours became shorter and the breaks longer. Now somewhat more complex products that required more time could be made. But since the workers worked as before in unified groups and shifts, these glassmaking works still had to be made in their breaks from work. Paperweights were best suited to the situation. A blob of glass was quickly taken from the oven, a few colorful bits of glass were taken, melted, pressed in, drawn out, colorful glass fibers were spun around, "combed", pressed in and squeezed again and finally covered once again by clear glass. All of this required only a few short, quick, practiced actions and another "letter-weight" was finished. Now it just needed to be removed neatly from the pontil and allowed to cool overnight.

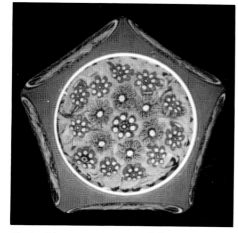

Red-white-green paperweight from Bohemia, 1845-55.

The better and more neatly the glowing glass was broken off the pontil, the less cutting and polishing had to be done under the bottom surface. For that reason, many fortunate examples of these old "Bohemian letter-weights" have their pontil mark on a somewhat concave surface, and its normally sharp edges thus did not scratch the surface under it. Other examples were later cut smooth underneath, and sometimes also polished. Not every glassworks possessed its own cutting equipment. For this purpose there were small specialist firms; cottage industries. But every glass-blower surely had contact with a glass refiner who cut and faceted his "letter-weights". Many of these letter-weights were struck, bumped or otherwise damaged over the years, so they surely had to be recut many times. They exist as smooth round, high, oval or wide, flat "balls" or cut with a wide variety of facets.

The numbers and types of decorations set into these letter-weights are almost infinite. In addition to colored bits of trim and glass fibers, metal wires (usually copper), air bubbles, quartz sand, and at times even simple millefiori pieces (especially in those made in Thuringia), and flowers and leaves made in advance on the glass-blowers' lamps were pressed into the letter-weights. Particularly pretty types were decorated with twisted and multicolored glass fibers. Some of these were even twisted into ornaments and snail figures and arranged very decoratively in the glass balls. Sometimes first names or family names made of glass canes were inlaid or modeled of bent copper wire, often including complete dedications, greetings and dates. Pressings or porcelain-paste or plaster castings of animals, ornaments, figures, medals or faces on porcelain plates were melted in. These very rare letter-weights with their extensive, complicated flower arrangements are especially charming and very costly. The flowers were made by the same laborious technique as was mastered circa 1850 at Clichy, Baccarat and Saint-Louis in France and is used today by only the world's best glass artists in America and France.

Although the glass experts in museums are not yet certain as to where the above mentioned masterworks were actually produced, it can still be said that they should be ranked among the "friggers". They turn up—if at all—only as unique pieces and can perhaps be regarded as contract work, trainee work or masterpieces.

The authors have seen these superb works only three times to date: at the Corning

Glass Museum in the USA, in a special exhibition at the Kunstgewerbemuseum in Vienna as a loan from a private owner, and in a German private collection.

The collector of this very unique type of letter-weight, a type of folk art from the turn of the century to somewhat before 1945 when the entire glass industry in these regions was nationalized, will be able to discover new motifs, cuts and types again and again. But he should also know that very similar, comparable work was produced during breaks by the workers in almost all the glassworks of central and northern Europe and given away or kept as souvenirs. Such pieces are particularly well known in Westphalia, southern Germany and Switzerland, as well as in all of Belgium and central and northern France. Such work has also come from Hungary, Rumania and Bulgaria, especially in the German settlements there, and it is worth noting that they are coming again today. Belgium and Italy too, along with the glassworks of Thuringia and Bohemia, are also in production again. Not as before, when it was only chance or break work allowed by the glassworks owners; today it is deliberate production, often entering the world of commerce via flea markets and appearing later at art auctions and in antique shops.

Almost all of these creations are very difficult, or even impossible, to differentiate. Only the very experienced and practiced glass collector can exercise the greatest foresight and care to protect himself from serious mistakes. But when deception was intended, even the best expert is not always safe. The outer form and "signs of wear" help him very little, and the tints of the glass and the glass colors are not much more helpful. More definite criteria can include the weight when the size is the same, and the complexity and delicacy of the inlays at a certain specified price. Information from dependable family members who can describe the history of the object as a long-standing family possession, are of more value. A particularly critical situation, and surely not a transitory one, is that of the "copying" trade in eastern Asia.

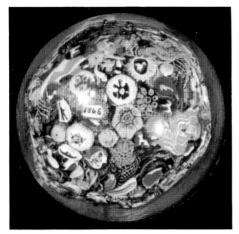

*Pietro Bigaglia paperweight,
1846.*

Murano: Scrambled weight, 1846.

Murano—Venice (circa 1840 to date)

In the period around 1840, just three names appear in the literature as possible producers of colorful glassware and glass beads, as well as millefiori glass: Pietro Bigaglia, Giovanni B. Franchini and Domenico Bussolin. The glass industry in Murano seems to have fallen to a commercial low point at that time. Only very little glass work from this period is known at all. All imaginable utensils were made of millefiori glass. Many kinds of millefiori and filigree canes as well as silhouette canes and aventurine glass have been used in tableware handles, bowls, chests, jewelry boxes, phials, and paperweights. In all these objects there is only a random, scrambled mixture of colorful glass-cane fragments. The glass pieces were broken freehand in various sizes, and often stretched and twisted while being melted in. The bits of canes are never arranged just on the surface; the glass ball is always completely filled with them. Only a thin layer of clear glass overlies the enclosed millefiori glasses, which may also be absent. The magnifying effect of a hemisphere of glass, commonly utilized in France and Bohemia, was not used here.

Only a very few of these Italian paperweights from the early years are known. It can thus be concluded that production must have been meager. Individual examples of these few paperweights are signed. A particularly beautiful and noteworthy feature of these somewhat curious-looking glass balls is the use of pretty silhouette canes, the faces, animal silhouettes, Venetian gondolas and, as mentioned, occasionally also monograms and dates. For example, "P. B. 1845" for Pietro Bigaglia. But this is, as noted, very rare. The selection of millefiori canes from Murano appears to be infinite. It must be kept in mind that Murano was once the center of glass production for the whole world and that millefiori-cane production in glassworks that specialized in them was routinely done in very great quantities. Millefiori glass was once available at every glassworks in Murano.

Since the 1850's, more names turn up as makers of glass beads and millefiori glass. One must remember that Murano still ranked second to Bohemia as a worldwide glass-bead producer. So it can be assumed that even in the twenties and thirties of this century—surely only in individual cases—millefiori paperweights were made in Murano.

But only since the renaissance of the paperweight after World War II began—inspired by the well-known paperweight collector Paul Jokelsen, founder of the American Paperweight Club at the beginning of the 1950's—has real mass-production taken place at Murano, flooding the worldwide souvenir market with paperweights in the very lowest price ranges. Notable among the successful glassworks are A.L.T. and Ferro & Lazzarini, as previously Moretti & Fratelli and Fratelli Toso.

Venice stands out as probably the world's greatest marketplace for glass. It has what appears to be an infinitely great ability to absorb these practical and low-priced mass-produced goods that have attracted so many glass collectors to genuine and valuable paperweights.

As with all genuine and valuable creations in this world, the imitations that they have inspired have scored the quantitatively greater success. But it seems in this case that the two surviving glassworks have also achieved great commercial success, since both of them have existed for many decades almost exclusively for the mass-production of paperweights. The worldwide demand for low-priced paperweights seems to remain endless. But the serious collector can also find, purely by chance, well-made masterworks among the many thousands of paperweights—works that are so harmonious and artistic in terms of color, composition, organization and production that they are worthy of inclusion in a paperweight collection.

From this new mass-production of Murano, which is intended primarily as souvenirs for tourists in Venice, and which has meanwhile resulted in a worldwide glut of cheap paperweights, there has also developed a market for "fakes" as well. They appear regularly at flea markets and the like, in antique shops, and even at art and antique auctions. The new Murano paperweights are made so differently from the classic paperweights that no one even halfway interested in genuine paperweights would be taken in by these inexpensive mass-produced articles.

Their prices range from $30 to $90 on the retail market.

Baccarat (1764 to date)

The "Compagnie des Cristalleries de Baccarat" is a large, important producer of the finest glasses, vases and other objects of lead crystal. Along with Saint-Louis, it is one of the two classic crystal works in France. It was founded at Baccarat in 1764 by the Bishop of Metz, Monseigneur de Montmorency-Laval, under the patronage of King Louis XV.

Lead-crystal glass has been used at Baccarat only since 1816. The production of classic paperweights began at Baccarat in 1846 and lasted only ten years. After 1856 there is no documentation that indicates further production of paperweights.

After no paperweights had been made at Baccarat for almost a hundred years—with brief interruptions during the two World Wars—the first, completely new experiments began forty years ago on the initiative of the American collector Paul Jokelson. When the church in Baccarat that was destroyed during the war was being dismantled in 1951, an old millefiori paperweight dated 1853 awakened interest in the resumption of paperweight production.

Work started at first with the less complicated technique, the melting-in of sulphides (porcelain-paste medallions). At the request of Paul Jokelson, the first choice was the portrait of the victorious American General, Dwight D. Eisenhower. These first attempts were not very successful. But the second sulphide paperweight, made in 1953 for the coronation of Queen Elizabeth II, was a success. Only in 1957, after many experiments, could millefiori paperweights be made by Baccarat in Baccarat again.

Baccarat-Signet

*Baccarat signet
"In admiration of the perfection and beauty of the work": Inscription by Louis XVIII in the guestbook of La Compagnie des Cristalleries de Baccarat, 1815.*

Photo: The glassworks at the foot of the French Vosges Mountains. Today it is the factory museum.

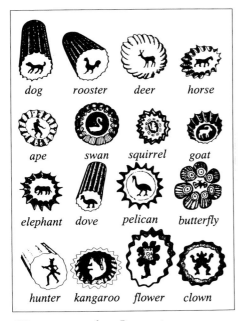

Silhouette canes from Baccarat.

Thanks to the great experience and technical facilities of this crystal works, all the techniques of paperweight production have been mastered very well. Masterful lampwork is produced, as are wondrously beautiful millefiori paperweights and good overlay paperweights, as well as simple sulphides.

The many different millefiori canes made in the sixties and seventies are particularly outstanding Baccarat products. As of 1971, for a period of some ten years, there appeared a series of paperweights with old Gridel motifs that were particularly characteristic of Baccarat. There are eighteen motifs in all, melted into millefiori paperweights. The main motif is always a large silhouette in the center, surrounded by a circle of all eighteen silhouettes. In betweem them, filling the entire bottom, are many hundreds of colorful millefiori canes. Every different motif is made in different patterns and colors.

Special Gridel issues by Baccarat since 1971 are:
1971: Rooster, 1972: Squirrel (1971), 1973: Elephant (1974), 1973: Horse, 1974: Pelican, 1974: Swan, 1974: Hunter, 1975: Turtle Doves, 1975: Pheasant, 1975: Black Ape, 1976: Deer, 1976: White Ape, 1977: Red Devil, 1977: Stork, 1978: Dog, 1978: Goat, 1979: Butterfly, 1979: Carrier Pigeon.

Clichy (1837-1870)

This is the third of the great French crystal works, whose name lives on today thanks to its works in the realm of paperweights made in the middle of the past century.

Founded at Billancourt near Paris in 1837, it was moved a short time later to Clichy-la-Garenne, then a suburb of Paris. It was not long before the paperweights made in this crystal works were in demand in the shops in Paris. As early as 1849 the crystal works at Saint-Louis were informed by a Paris dealer that Clichy could not deliver as many paperweights as were wanted.

As is known today, the production of good paperweights is very time-consuming. But it is still more time-consuming to find capable glass-blowers and train them to be even better paperweight makers. This has not changed from that day to this. There is yet another difficulty involved. Glass-blowers and glassmakers do not necessarily have to have a great deal of patience and care for their profession. Those are not the main requirements that are asked of good glass-blowers, who were then much more numerous than they are now. But for good paperweight makers, these are the two most important requirements for the production of the very best paperweights.

The external ball shape, the profile of the Clichy paperweight, was originally high and round. During the course of the last 150 years, it could well have changed owners and suffered damage to its glass surface. Scratches, cracks, splinters, rough spots and even deep holes often detracted from the originally highly polished and mirror-smooth paperweight. By cutting and polishing the surface anew, owners sought to improve their paperweights, which had by then become valuable rarities. Thus the paperweights became smaller and flatter from time to time, and no longer show the original profile or the original cut.

The great majority of the paperweights made at Clichy, like those of all the other manufacturers, were almost perfectly round, with only the appropriate differences in profile. Only the bottom was cut "hollow", so that a rim of barely visible width, up to a few millimeters, was formed. More and more such paperweights turn up in which the base is cut flat (with only a few exceptions, this is the original cut, such as that of the millefiori overlay mushroom of Clichy). The upper arch of the ball is no longer round but nearly flat, and various decorative cuts appear, making the paperweights look strange. In all these cases there was damage that was repaired by cutting and polishing. This can often be done expertly, so that a decrease in value does not necessarily result.

The desirable Clichy spiral paperweights (swirls) appear especially flat, most of them having been cut that way later. This motif was made exclusively at Clichy in the middle of the past century. The spirals run outward from the center to both the left and right. The spiral canes were set into the colors alternatingly. Often they have only two colors. To conceal the point at which the spirals come together unbecomingly in the center, there is always a millefiori cane, a so-called "pastry mold cane." More rarely the famous Clichy rose appears here in a variety of colors: red, pink, white and green.

Special Clichy paperweights show not only the complicated, complex and thick millefiori canes also used by Baccarat and Saint-Louis, but also canes that look quite simple in cross-section. They look like several batter molds, one inside the other, such as are used to bake cookies. Hence their name of pastry mold canes.

The paperweight makers of Clichy must have had particular difficulties with the various colored glasses and the overlaying of the "Teppichgrund" motif (carpet ground paperweights), as well as the filigree and "Körbchen"" (basket) types. Again and again one comes upon Clichy paperweights that have in their lower third a partially or completely encircling hairline crack that a fingernail can feel. The danger of these paperweights finally breaking apart one day is not very great if the object has already lasted 50, 100 or even 150 years with this crack. It cannot be determined when these cracks appear or have appeared.

Clichy presumably produced the greatest numbers of all French paperweights. A total of about 10,000 pieces seems realistic.

The technique of paperweight production was also utilized in the production of crystal-ball sets of bedknobs and banister posts, doorknobs and window handles, carafes, perfume bottles and vases. The millefiori canes could be placed in the bottoms and the stoppers of the hollow glassware.

After 1870 (and the Franco-Prussian War), no further paperweight production is known. The glassworks were taken over by the crystal works of Sèvres, which had meanwhile become more influential. Since then, the name of Clichy appeared only for a short time in the combined name "Cristallerie de Sèvres et Clichy." Today a crystal works with the name "Cristallerie de Sèvres" exists again at Sevres, near Paris. The traditional ties to Clichy, though, have been broken off. Similar production has not been taken up.

Silhouette canes from Clichy. Above is the renowned and rare Clichy Rose.

The glass works of Saint-Louis in the mid-nineteenth century, the high point of paperweight production.

Saint-Louis (1767 to date)

Like Baccarat, Saint-Louis is one of the two classic crystal works of France. The factory is an important producer of the finest cut and often gilded glasses, vases and other objects made of lead crystal. It was founded in 1767 under the patronage of the French King Louis XV. The "Royal Glassworks" of Saint-Louis can presently trace its history back to 1586, when the original glassworks were founded at that locality in the Argenthal region. The "Compagnie des Cristalleries de Saint-Louis" is today one of the world's most prestigious glassworks. It is certainly the most successful in the production of paperweights. After a hiatus of almost a hundred years, the production of paperweights was resumed in 1953, with the encouragement of the Franco-American Paul Jokelson of New York. His urging to redevelop the old paperweight techniques were accepted enthusiastically by the sales director Gérard Ingold, then still a young man, so in the same year a paperweight with a portrait of Queen Elizabeth II appeared on the occasion of her coronation.

Most paperweights are made according to chosen classic nineteenth-century designs. Saint-Louis shows flowers in great variety, many different kinds of fruit, colorful spirals, complicated baskets and interesting lizards. All the techniques of paperweight production, such as lamp work, millefiori, filigree and overlay, were mastered perfectly. Paperweights with gold foil medallions represent a new type of production.

Since older Saint-Louis paperweights bring the highest prices at auctions, the greatest importance is now placed on producing only first-class examples.

All Saint-Louis paperweights are marked with the initials "SL" and the year. The series are limited to small quantities of 150 to an average of 300 and a maximum of 600 for the entire world. A certificate of authenticity accompanies every paperweight. Since 1990, all paperweights have had numbers engraved on their bases.

Signets and trade marks from Saint-Louis, France, from 1767 to the present.

Initials "SL" from Saint-Louis, France.

Pantin (1850-1890)

Only since about thirty years ago can some previously unidentified French paperweights be ascribed to a small glassworks near Paris, Monot & Cie. by name, which was founded in 1850 in what was then the suburb and now the city district of Pantin on the Seine. As with the other three French paperweight manufacturers, the town in which it was located gave its name to the glassworks.

It is certain that, unlike the other three crystal works, Pantin never made great quantities of paperweights. Also, Pantin paperweights show a completely different signature than those previously known. This was not an important crystal-glassworks, and its chief production program was devoted much less to the area of decorative and table crystal than was the case at its competitor Clichy, but rather in the area of technical glass for the chemical industry.

Thus it is not surprising that in this glassworks outstanding paperweights were produced through complexly created lampwork. For a long time no one could imagine who could have been able to produce them at that time. On the one hand, this is an explanation for the finely made, striking paperweights, but on the other hand it is also a reason why so few examples exist and the prices are always very high.

The famous "caterpillars on the leaf" paperweight is likewise a good example of Pantin paperweights, as are the larger and more complex salamander weights. For these paperweights, the salamanders were first modeled individually before melting in, and then worked cold. The numerous overlays of colored glass were partially cut through and polished on the smallest copper wheels (copper-wheel engraving), giving the salamanders a wide variety of designs. Only afterward could the salamander be reheated, made almost liquid, and then melted into the paperweight along with all the other decorations.

This laborious work has been brought back to life recently in America by Delmo Tarsitano with his big lizard, snake and salamander paperweights (see "Independent Artists"). More recently, Victor Trabucco has also offered Gila monsters.

In addition, many flowers and fruits are found in Pantin products, above all especially big and beautiful roses. The blossoms and leaves are formed to look extraordinarily natural. The colors are modest and understated; they are by no means exaggerated, glaring or brilliant.

Whenever Pantin paperweights appear at auctions, they always attract the greatest attention and the highest prices. Since they basically fit into the era after Clichy, Baccarat and Saint-Louis, their production probably took place in the years between 1870 and 1880.

Whitefriars (1680-1980)

Whitefriars of London, founded in 1680, ranked along with Baccarat and Saint-Louis in France as the only glassworks that still mastered or had re-learned the classic manner of millefiori paperweight production in our times. In the realm of millefiori paperweights, Whitefriars was definitely in the lead in terms of fine precision work.

In 1834 a glassmaker from Bristol, James Powell, bought a glassworks in London and carried on the business under the name of J. Powell and Sons. Later in the same decade, the glassworks moved from the shore of the Thames in inner London to the suburb of Wealdstone, to be carried on there until 1962 under the name of Powell. Only as of 1962—after the last of the five Powell generations who ran the Whitefriars firm died—did the name of Whitefriars reappear in Whitefriars Glass Ltd. Only from this point on was paperweight production apparently taken up intensively again. Although Whitefriars produced several hundred paperweights a year from then until the kilns were shut down in 1980, the constantly growing demand could not be met. In 1980 Whitefriars had to halt production permanently, as it no longer showed a profit. Meanwhile the property to which the glassworks had been moved from central London to a suburb had become so expensive that the land was sold for economic reasons and the glassworks went out of business. All the paperweights made by the firm to 1980 are marked with the blue millefiori symbol of a stylized white-garbed monk (White Friars) and the year.

Whitefriars paperweights can also be distinguished from those of other manufacturers by their characteristic bases. Whitefriars always had its very own production method, and the paperweights look as if the bottoms are open. All Whitefriars paperweights are made of lead crystal and typically brilliant and heavy.

Because of the many different motifs, no great quantities were made. Every example differs from every other, even if it has the same catalog number. Every object is an individual piece. The variety of the different cuts is typical of Whitefriars; it was a glassworks at which all glasses were cut complexly and with many facets.

There is still a so-called Whitefriars Collection on the market today. Several motifs are issued every year. They are made, though, by the Caithness Glass Ltd. group of firms in Scotland. This company purchased not only many glassmaking tools, raw glass and glass recipes but also the firm's name and "White Friar" trade mark when the Whitefriars firm closed down in 1980. Thus the original symbol of the white friar can be used legally. All new "Whitefriars" paperweights made by Caithness since 1980 bear this symbol and the year, 1981 or later.

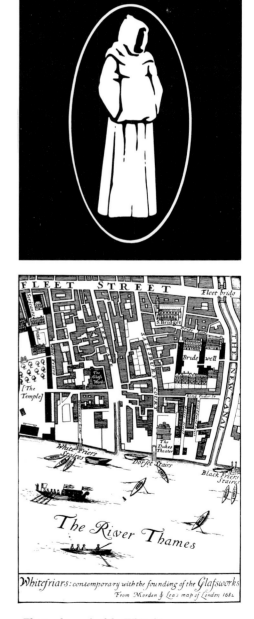

The trade mark of the Whitefriars firm and a historical map showing its location in London.

These paperweights no longer have anything in common with the genuine millefiori lead-crystal paperweights made by Whitefriars, other than this small monk symbol. Never in its 300-year history did Whitefriars produce lampwork paperweights, as Caithness does today. These Caithness paperweights are frequently smaller and not as heavy as the Whitefriars originals, since they are not made of lead crystal.

History says nothing about old Whitefriars paperweights from the past century. Many experts even assume that Whitefriars paperweights turned up in the 1930's as fakes, marked with the date 1848 and made by some other British glassworks. It cannot be determined with certainty whether Whitefriars had made any millefiori paperweights before 1930. If they did, they could have only been individual pieces, for old Whitefriars paperweights are practically never seen on the market.

Valuable and typical millefiori paperweights from Whitefriars, London.

Bacchus (circa 1850)

After many name changes, Bacchus & Sons was the last name borne by this firm in Birmingham, England, before it closed down prior to the turn of the century. Birmingham ranks with Stourbridge as a center of the British glass industry. Since there was always strong competition with imported Bohemian glass in Britain, it was natural to use those products as models. This explains why millefiori decorations turned up individually on utilitarian glassware such as vases, phials and other household glass. This cannot have been done to any great degree, since only relatively few millefiori paperweights have been attributed to the Bacchus firm.

These paperweights are especially large and—if not cut at a later date—especially high and round, almost eight centimeters in diameter. The relatively coarse, unvaried millefiori pattern is usually laid out in concentric circles. Along with many simple, thick glass canes (pastry mold canes, similar to those from Clichy), there are also individual complex, combined canes to be found. Many of the canes appear to be hollow. The colors are often pale and light, since considerably more white was used as a "color" than was used in France.

Perthshire (1968 to date)

These paperweights are made by hand in a small Scottish glassworks which has taken on the task of perfecting the production of paperweights with a great deal of skill and special techniques. The very limited yearly special editions are almost always combinations of many paperweight techniques; thus they are laboriously made. A particular characteristic of the Perthshire paperweights is the small and very varied silhouette canes that have been used often since 1972.

Very noteworthy and rarely achieved by other paperweight producers with such perfection and regularity is the external shape of the paperweights. They are always almost perfectly round, smooth and highly sparkling, and at the top they never show any irregularity in the glass. Only the bottom, the base, is a weak point in Perthshire paperweights. It is often carelessly cut, and seldom polished to a high gloss.

New and very varied millefiori motifs in many colors are always to be seen in the firm's reasonably priced, unlimited standard offerings. The "P" cane can be found in many paperweights, and the limited editions also show the date.

Perthshire developed from the earlier firms of Vasart and Strathearn Glass in Scotland, both of which were managed by Stuart Drysdale, the founder of Perthshire Paperweights Ltd. In both of these firms, first at Vasart Glass (Ysart family) in the fifties and sixties, later at Strathearn Glass until about the beginning of the seventies, paperweights were produced using the traditional millefiori technique on a colorful background of croze bits.

When paperweight construction began at Perthshire Glass, the products of the three different glassworks in the region could scarcely be told apart. Since many of the workers had moved to Perthshire Glass, this is easily explained. The similarity of earlier millefiori paperweights made by Caithness to those made by Vasart and Strathearn likewise is based on the relocation of glass-blowers. And everywhere there appeared the easily recognized handwriting of the Scottish master and well-known paperweight pioneer Paul Ysart (see the following).

The founder of Perthshire Glass, Stuart Drysdale, died in 1990. His son directs the company now.

Paul Ysart

Pablo (Paul) Moreno Ysart was born into a glassmaking family in Barcelona in 1904. His father, Salvador, and his grandfather were both glass-blowers. Paul Ysart qualifies today as one of the most important people in the new development of the old paperweight techniques in this century. From Scotland, to which his family emigrated with him in 1914-15 after a brief stay in France, he was a pioneer of glassmaking and artistic glass-blowing. He had learned them expertly from his father.

Even before World War II, and soon after it again, Paul Ysart mastered both the millefiori and the lampwork techniques excellently. A vast array of the most varied motifs, such as flowers, dragonflies, butterflies, snakes, birds and fish, combined with or without millefiori, filigree, and usually one-color or multicolored croze backgrounds, were produced by him. His working life extended until he was more than 75 years old. The Scottish glassworks of Moncrieff (Monart Glass) and Vasart Glass, both long since out of existence, were closely connected with the Ysarts. Wherever man has experimented with paperweights in Scotland, the name of Ysart turns up. The first initials of the brothers Vincent and Antoine and the name Ysart contributed to the name of Vasart. The paperweights made by Strathearn Glass were also based on the experiments of Paul Vasart. As of 1963 Paul Ysart took a position as director of training at the recently founded Caithness Glass firm in Wick, in northern Scotland. Here he produced paperweights himself, and they were also produced under his direction. Many classic, traditional paperweights made by him personally or under his direction at Caithness from the mid-sixties to about the end of 1970, usually in spare time after regular work was over, are signed with an "H" cane. Immediately after his retirement—he was already 66 years old—Paul Ysart again began a career in 1971 as an independent paperweight artist. He may well have worked at Caithness Glass from time to time too. But P. Y. soon founded his own glass studio. He operated at first in the lighthouse at Wick-Harland (as Harland Glass), later as P. Y. Glass Co., and then in 1977 as Highland Paperweights. All the very good paperweights made by him from 1970 to about 1979-80—and they remained identical in terms of style—are signed with a "PY" cane. These paperweights were distributed by the American paperweight dealer and well-known paperweight pioneer Paul Jokelson of New York. The simpler ones still bore the "H" initial.

In the last few years, many fake paperweights signed "PY" have appeared all over Great Britain, and can be recognized only with difficulty by the slightly changed "PY" initials.

The Spaniard Paul Ysart, who became world-famous through his master craftsmanship in the production of traditional paperweights in Scotland and left his legacy of the modern paperweight in his students, died at the end of 1991 at the age of almost 88.

Caithness Glass (1969 to date)

The glassmaking firm of Caithness Glass Ltd. was founded in northernmost Scotland in 1960. Since 1969 modern, usually abstract and futuristic-looking paperweights have been produced. Free and unburdened by the classic paperweight production of the past, the Caithness glassmakers have succeeded in astounding the admirers of these new-generation paperweights again and again with imaginative, mysterious motifs.

The traditional millefiori and lampwork paperweights of Paul Ysart (at Caithness 1963-1970) are signed with an "H" cane. Since 1970 the firm's millefiori paperweights have been signed with a "CG" cane.

Caithness Glass is the firm where two paperweight artists Peter Holmes and William Manson—as young men in the sixties—learned the techniques of creating almost all kinds of paperweights from the famous master Paul Ysart. Peter Holmes is now the proprietor of Selkirk Glass Ltd. His paperweights have meanwhile become competitors to those of Caithness.

William Manson is likewise not employed by Caithness Glass any more. But he is still active for Caithness, though now (as of 1992) on a free lance basis. All expensive, naturalistic lampwork paperweights with salamanders, fish, snakes and other animals, as well as with plants, are almost without exception the works of glass artist William Manson. They are always made in very small quantities: 25, 50 or 100 pieces. All of them are signed, numbered, and etched with "Caithness Glass" on the base.

Although the glass used by Caithness is not ideally suited for cutting and polishing, a good many paperweights are sharply cut to achieve special effects and light refraction. Colin Terris has been the firm's designer since 1968.

Under the brand name of "Whitefriars", and with the symbol and date, Caithness has produced small cut lampwork paperweights combined with millefiori since 1981. They have nothing in common with the original Whitefriars paperweights that were produced in the London area until 1980.

Selkirk Glass (1977 to date)

The owners of this new, modern glassworks are Peter Holmes and Ron Hutchison, two former Caithness Glass employees. Only since 1977 have Peter Holmes and his young team been producing the most modern paperweights at his own glassworks in southern Scotland. Since his sixteenth birthday, Peter Holmes studied glassmaking, glass-blowing and particularly paperweight production at the best-known Scottish glassworks, Caithness Glass. He was first an apprentice, later an assistant to the master of twentieth-century paperweight production, Paul Ysart. While he was still at Caithness, his work began to attract the attention of glass and paperweight collectors. Along with the traditional (French) paperweight techniques, he has mastered in superb style the production of all abstract, free-formed motifs. His imaginative, futuristic motifs are usually produced in limited editions, numbered to a maximum of 500 pieces, and signed. Such names as Space Orbit, Equinox, Saturn or Silver Rhapsody are chosen for them, and more than eighty different motifs are always available for the collector. Many special editions for private individuals, and particularly for the proprietors of firms, have appeared. All works not only designed by Peter Holmes and developed for production by his team, but also created personally by him, are marked with a PH signature cane, usually in the base. It is also worthy of note that the glass of the modern Selkirk paperweights is light and brilliant in its luster and almost crystal-clear. The prices range from 100 to about $240.

"J" Glass by John Deacons (1979-1983, 1987 to date)

"J" Glass (also "Jay" Glass) is the finest handcrafted art from a very small Scottish glassworks. The owner, John Deacons, has long since perfected the handicraft of paperweight making. He has mastered all the techniques of the glassmaking craft, but prefers flower motifs made in lampwork. A noteworthy designer and glass-blower in his team until 1983 was young Alan Scott, who now works for Caithness Glass in Perth.

In this small factory, the highest standards for a variety-rich and valuable array of products are met. A particularly striking feature of the firm's paperweights is the perfection with which they are made.

As a sign of their authenticity and uniqueness, all paperweights are marked by a "J" in the glass. Every paperweight is accompanied by a numbered and signed certificate. Each motif was limited to a worldwide total of 101 pieces until 1983.

Since the new beginning in 1987, only millefiori paperweights in somewhat larger quantities have been made; they are unlimited. The few lampwork paperweights that are made are single pieces. John Deacons works completely alone today. His production rarely rises higher than one or two dozen paperweights a month.

Another signature used on paperweights by John Deacons is a white cane with a green or blue thistle and the year.

China (1930 to date)

In the 1930's the first paperweights from China appeared. Clever American business people had already recognized the trend toward collecting the hard-to-manufacture "glass balls." They wanted to do a good business, so they took genuine old French paperweights of the past century to Chinese glassworks and had them copied.

So it is not surprising that only a few, some eight to ten old motifs, appear today. Among them is Baccarat's pansy motif, and its repeating millefiori patterns are formed and placed with a lack of expertise. All Chinese paperweights of this time are relatively small, only about six centimeters in diameter. They are flat and made of poor-quality glass. This is understandable, for China had neither a glass-blowing tradition nor paperweights made of glass. The true spirit of collecting that the old French works of glass art inspired among Americans and central Europeans was not recognized here.

All paperweights were then, as again today, marked for export with an adhesive paper label reading "Made in China." A few examples also have this lettering set into the glass.

Since 1970, China has begun to export paperweights again. The modern motifs, unlike the pre-war models, show originality. Again and again there are very special Chinese flower concepts, such as a type of spider chrysanthemum in various colors. Today the paperweights are no longer flat, but very highly arched, almost completely round, or egg-shaped. The glass, though, is still of the simplest quality.

It is typical of Chinese glass, as it was for many types from Murano, that the moisture in the air brings about a chemical reaction that leads to the formation of acetic acid. If the paperweights are not wiped off for some time, many of them smell strongly of vinegar, which does not happen with the presently known crystal glass from central Europe. The colors are in part "typically" Chinese, including white, Chinese red, a bright yellow, orange, green and a satiated, clear blue. The base, often very small, usually looks dull and irregular, only moderately concave and partly eroded away in its original condition. Recently, German business people have gone to China, as Americans did in the thirties, to teach American paperweight techniques to the Chinese glass-blowers. As of the present, they are supposed to copy the California glass artists and deliver their goods at very low prices. The serious paperweight collector will probably find no joy in these primitive mass-produced copies of original works of art. The short period of China's own original glass creations thus seems to have come to an end. These earlier, sometimes very pretty paperweights are already being sold in shops and discount houses for prices from $3 to $25. The new mass-produced Chinese copies of American glass art, on the other hand, are more expensive.

America (1850-1895)

Around the middle of the past century, at the time of the greatest wave of immigration that the USA ever experienced, the most beautiful paperweights were being produced in the French glassworks. At the same time, though, hundreds of thousands of Europeans were emigrating to America, including English, Irish, Germans and Italians as well as many French, most of whom left their homeland in great poverty. Revolutions, uprisings and wars were taking place in large areas of Europe. The unrest and the social upheavals that resulted provided the impetus to emigrate. America was the answer to peace and freedom.

The American glass industry developed more strongly because of the growing population and at first produced the products that were known from Europe. The immigrant glass-blowers could thus continue their handiwork in the same form with the same techniques. Many came from the French crystal works of Baccarat and Saint-Louis, and they surely brought recipes in their heads, samples of colorful glass canes and tools in their pockets. Soon after the exposition at the Crystal Palace in London, the first American paperweights appeared, made by the New England Glass Company from 1851 on. They were not the frigger paperweights, but regular trade goods, comparable with the products of Clichy, Baccarat and Saint-Louis.

Along with the NEGC, Sandwich Glass, Cambridge Glass, Pairpoint Glass, the Cape Cod Glass Company, Mount Washington Glass Company, Franklin Flint Glass Works and later Gillinder and Sond were in operation. These glassworks, most of them located very close to each other on the Atlantic coast of America, almost became "relatives" thanks to many changes of ownership, reorganizations, mergers, name changes and closings over the years. In the chronology of the glassworks, the same English and, in particular, Alsatian-French names turn up regularly as directors and glassmakers: Denning Jarves, John Hopkins, Thomas Leighton from Britain, François Pierre from Baccarat and William T. Gillinder, William Libbey, Michael Owens and Nicholas Lutz from Saint-Louis, France.

Almost all the paperweights that were produced then, in only small quantities, strongly resembled the French products. Some are dated, the earliest date being 1852. Flowers made by lampwork showed just as much skill as many varieties of millefiori. Heavy high-lead crystal glass was worked along with lighter low-lead crystal and simple crystal glass.

Outstanding among American paperweight production are the hollow blown fruit paperweights, and most particularly the large petaled rose paperweights made by the Mt. Washington Glass Company. One suspects that these masterworks were made only toward the end of the century, about a hundred years ago, by the master Nicholas Lutz from Saint-Louis. Lutz worked at Mt. Washington until 1895. These rose paperweights are known to exist in pink, red, yellow and blue. Much that is unknown in the past history of these unique rose paperweights (as well as plaquettes or flat letter-weights, made in the same manner) will unfortunately never be known again.

South of the New England states, where most of the American glassworks were originally located, the glass industry had also developed early in Millville, New Jersey. Presumably the glass-blowers from France were missing. Completely different techniques for making paperweights were developed in Millville; the Millville rose paperweights are typical of this area. These paperweights always show a thick, almost complete rose blossom, mostly in red and yellow overlay colors on white glass in the middle of the almost spherical paperweight. At the place where the thick rose petals are melted together at the base there are two or three green leaves, likewise very thick. The spherical paperweight is often fitted with a base. In these lovely Millville roses, the petals seem to be melted together as lampwork—but it only looks that way. In this simple, comparatively crude work, the petal divisions were first pressed into a red- or yellow-overlaid glass ball with a rough iron tool. These impressions divided the individual petals. After that, the rose was pressed forward, pushed into the glass, and covered with clear glass.

In the glassworks in the Millville area, new creations appeared with a graphic pattern, a drawn picture, a signature or a combination of these inside. To make them, iron forms were first made and the patterns machined into them in negative form. Then white or colored glass powder or glass granules were sprinkled into the form as the desired effect required, and then a ball of molten glass was poured over them. The "powdered glass picture" melted with the fluid glass and was lifted with it out of the negative form. A glass carrier could then let another ball of glass fall onto the picture from above. Turned briefly in the wet wooden model, the paperweight was formed quickly. These paperweights could be produced very quickly and economically. They were used mainly for advertising. Almost every American business had its logo immortalized in paperweights at that time. Coca-Cola is only one example of the many names that turn up again and again in paperweights. They were genuine letter-weights then, made for practical use. The industry is still located in Millville and still produces this type of letter-weight on request.

The Glass Studios

Studio-Glass Paperweights

The small glass studios of America are still a rather new variety of artistic workshop, somewhere between the big industrial glassworks with their big melting kilns on the one hand and the individual glass artists on the other hand, who almost always work without any glass-melting kiln. They go back only 20 to 25 years and have scarcely appeared in Europe to date.

In an industrial glassworks or a smaller crystal factory, a glass artist can scarcely give free rein to his imagination without liquid glass. On the other hand, the individual glass artist does without the medium of liquid glass altogether and dedicates himself exclusively to the various traditional cold-glass arts such as glass painting or the artistic working of glass by cutting and polishing, sandblasting or etching.

Here the development and technical perfection of small glass-melting kilns, as well as their heating, insulating and control, offered a solution long awaited by many. Painters, sculptors, ceramic and glass artists in particular, who wanted to work and create freely with liquid glass (hot glass), were excited when the first studio glass kilns were demonstrated, at first at colleges and universities. This was the beginning of the studio-glass movement, and completely new, often unique works of glass art have been created since then.

Almost all of the artists who work in these modern glass studios were introduced to the small glass-melting kilns previously when they were in college and used them within the framework of their art training.

The paperweights that are made in these studios show all the existing production techniques. The new technique of painting on hot glass developed only in the past twenty years and has been named the California paperweight technique, after its place of origin. It is also demonstrated on large glass objects as well as the smallest glass phials.

With this glass and technique, the artist has almost 100% freedom to form his objects as he wishes. In extreme cases, he can keep the glass liquid for hours and thus paint the most beautiful pictures, like a painter, very slowly and carefully. The many glass colors (colored glass) are his formative medium, the glass from the melting kiln is his linen, the carrier of the color, and the iron spikes and forceps are his brushes. A "solvent" for the colors is at his disposal too—it is the flame of his constantly burning welding torch. With this torch he must keep the colored glass that is on the surface of the object liquid enough to paint with.

Examples of designs from Correia Art Glass.

Correia Art Glass

The American glass artist Steven Correia, grandson of Portuguese immigrants, founded his small glass studio in Los Angeles at the beginning of the seventies. After his departure in 1980, the studio was taken over, modernized and enlarged by his brother-in-law Efrem Zimbalist III, son of Efrem Zimbalist, Jr. In addition to iridescent glass vases and other objects in Tiffany style, such paperweights were also made. The best-known and most typical of Correia's paperweights are his completely new types, which have been made partly opaque on the outside by sandblasting, with their interior form visible only from an upward angle through a polished window. Enclosed in them, mostly in flat, two-dimensional pictorial technique, are colorful flowers, birds, fish and insects. These fine pieces of work, which were created by the present-day artist Chris Buzzini (see "Independent Artists") between 1982 and 1986 and before he went his own way, have become renowned and desired. Ken Rosenfeld (see "Independent Artists") also worked for Correia in the mid-eighties and learned the techniques of glassmaking there.

All Correia paperweights are signed with the Correia signature on the base and also bear a serial code number, sometimes an additional catalog number for the series-production paperweights, and the date, but never the name of an individual artist.

Abelman Art Glass

Since the beginning of the eighties Abelman Art Glass Studio has made all kinds of glassware in pink-gold-green-yellow-blue-iridescent Tiffany style. Since a short time ago, paperweights have also been part of the program, but to date they have all been opaque and iridescent on the surface. This glass studio is worth mentioning and considering for the paperweight collector only because of a new, young paperweight artist: Mayauel Ward (see "Independent Artists"). Self-taught, he has developed into an artist in the last four years. After just a short time, Mayauel Ward has learned all the paperweight techniques and is already modeling the most complicated flower and cactus paperweights. His rare early works, which he made exclusively as miniature paperweights because larger blocks of glass were not yet available to him at that time, are very much in demand.

Lotton Art Glass

At the beginning of the seventies, Charles Lotton of Chicago first came into contact with the glass art. He was probably the first glass artist in postwar America to produce a strongly iridescent lustrous sheen on his vases and objects. He produced chiefly the iridescent gold tulip lamp chimneys for genuine or copied Tiffany lamps.

At the beginning of the nineties, his three sons began to create freely designed glass objects. Along with Dave with his iridescent Tiffany-style paperweights, the youngest son, John, has been very successful with his magnum paperweights. John Lotton is presently the only glass artist in the world who has succeeded in making paperweights the size of a basketball. Using several transparent layers, one over another, and beginning with a fist-size nucleus, he models tendrils, leaves, garlands and blossoms, also one over another. The effect of depth when one looks through the tendrils is incredible and fascinating. Every one of his great works in glass is unique, and some of them weigh more than twenty kilograms. John Lotton can make only one of these super-magnums in a week, and the gigantic mass of glass must cool to room temperature for more than a week under strictly controlled conditions.

All Lotton works are engraved with the artist's signature.

Lundberg Studio Glass

James Lundberg, who was fatally injured in the spring of 1992, was the leader and driving force of the Lundberg Glass Studio in the USA. Steven, his younger brother, is a talented paperweight artist.

The brothers Daniel and David Salazar have been able to create their own very individual style alongside Steven Lundberg. Their paperweights are glass paintings. The pictorial work is created on and in the glowing glass ball, directly at the kiln, by the hands of these three glass artists. David has meanwhile become independent and prefers miniature paperweights that transfer the delicate motif nobly to the surface and make it tangible. The studio attained worldwide fame through James Lundberg's idea of modeling the earth accurately in glass as a globe. A look at our planet from a spacecraft, which is otherwise granted only to the astronauts! Every single Lundberg paperweight is marked with the name of the studio, that of the artist, the year and a registration number.

Above: Yellow dahlia by Steven Lundberg. Below: Chrysanthemums by Steven Lundberg.

Orient & Flume Art Glass

Orient & Flume began to produce paperweights in 1972 at a small studio in California, shortly after this community of artists had been founded in Chico, and in fact at the corner of Orient and Flume Streets.

A small group of artists has developed special ideas and unified them into a characteristic design. Typical of the Orient & Flume paperweights until into the eighties are those with motifs that, because of their iridescent surface decoration, resemble Art Nouveau. Out of the union of these elements with the traditional paperweight techniques there has arisen an unchanging style that characterizes this team of artists. Classic flower and animal motifs as well as millefiori are now included in their works, which include paperweights, vases, jewelry and other glass objects. The combing technique, brought to perfection here, ennobles almost every paperweight. The surface often seems to be velvety. Every piece is unique, and all are signed, numbered and dated.

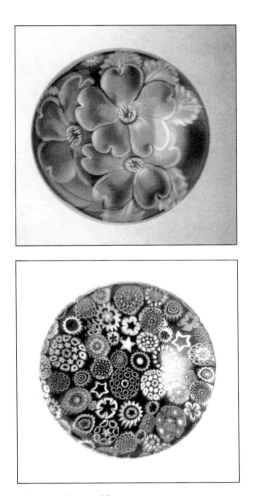

Above: Cherry-blossom paperweight. Below: Millefiori paperweight by Orient & Flume, USA.

Parabelle Glass

Gary and Doris Scrutton founded their own glass studio in Portland in 1983 and have devoted their work exclusively to the production of paperweights. Shortly before that, they had sold their glass dealership to their two grown sons. Thus they could concentrate on paperweights. They are particularly interested in French millefiori paperweights, especially those from Clichy. The Scruttons are the only paperweight artists in the world who make everything themselves. They form and draw not only all of their millefiori canes themselves, modeling them in their own iron molds, they also mix their colored-glass compositions to their own recipes; Doris Scrutton designs the patterns for the canes and the paperweights.

Their assortment of only five or six paperweights, new every year, is very limited, with only 75 to 100 pieces being made, and naturally soon sold out.

The millefiori canes are very varied and the patterns are drawn very accurately. A very striking feature of Parabelle Glass is the pansy silhouette cane that appears in many colors. All Parabelle paperweights are signed with a "PB" cane, the year and one or two small bells.

Josh Simpson Glass

The only one of America's paperweight artists who moved from free objective art to paperweights is Josh Simpson. Today he still remains an object artist whose glass artworks are admired in many of the world's museums.

Strictly speaking, his paperweights are not genuine paperweights in the sense of this book. His works that resemble paperweights, though, are made so imaginatively that they must at least be mentioned briefly here. In massive glass balls of every size, up to about twenty centimeters in diameter, Josh Simpson draws, paints, models, shapes, lays, presses and creates a fantasy world. A world that exists only in his artistic fantasy arises and is turned to reality in the paperweight. The observer feels transported to faraway stars or sunk into unknown oceans. His paperweight works are ideas solidified in glass. He calls them *Inhabited Planet, Perhaps Inhabited Planet, Mega-World.* All are signed, unique works.

Independent Artists

Lampwork Paperweights

With the great success of the paperweights from the two surviving great French crystal works of Saint-Louis and Baccarat some 25 years ago (late sixties/early seventies), especially in the USA, a completely new group of paperweight producers developed there in particular: the individual artists. They sit in their small workshops behind their "glass-blowers' lamps" and, patiently and with great skill, model small blossoms and leaves, stems, roots, fruits and moss out of thin staffs of colored glass; also included are all kinds of animals, from ants, bees, beetles, spiders and butterflies to snakes and salamanders to birds of all colors. Only when they have succeeded in creating these works, arrangements or bouquets can they proceed to put these portrayals, almost always three-dimensional, in and under clear blocks of glass.

All of these new glass artists utilize the so-called "glass-blower's lamp". They have no glass-melting kilns at their disposal from which they can take molten glass, as is done in the glassworks. Instead they have special round glass blocks that they have heated to a soft state in warming ovens, so they can imbed and melt in their delicate works of glass art. This extremely difficult work process is naturally done with great care. It requires the great ability to guarantee that the hours of preparation of the many tiny details will not be damaged, twisted or even destroyed while being melted in.

Almost without exception the best of these glass artists come from the realm of technical glassworking, glass equiptment or laboratoryglass making. They all know and admire the famous glass plant collection of the Blaschkas from Dresden of the past century in the museum at Harvard University in Boston, USA.

Because of the complexity involved in making a paperweight in this way and the enormous amount of time required, they can make only a very few examples during the course of a year. Two to three hundred pieces are sold out in no time. Many artists can make only fifty to sixty pieces. Their paperweights are unique creations, differing individually even when using the same motifs. This is understandable, as every single paperweight is conceived and modeled by the artist himself.

The interest in these unique paperweights never ends. Almost every year, a new glass artist emerges in the USA and delights collectors with his creations. Influential conditions have made it possible for most collectors' paperweights to come from the USA today. In addition to the clubs organized for paperweight collectors, there are numerous significant paperweight collections on permanent display in various American museums. There is much demand in Europe, but the inspiration is in America.

Setting up and opening a glass studio in a private home or in any neighborhood is allowed in the USA with hardly any limitations. There are practically no limits on artistic expression in any way. Budding artists come into contact with gas ovens in schools, colleges and universities. All the technical apparatus, equipment and raw glass are available everywhere at reasonable prices. We should not forget to mention a very important element: endless patience. The more care and patience the artist has, the more superb his paperweights will be. A light, quick overpainting is not possible in glaze art. Every decison, every motion, every brush stroke, must stay there once applied.

From the beginning (circa 1970), Paul Stankard, Ray Banford, his son Bob and Francis Whittemore have been at work. But Charles Kaziun was the pioneer of this generation of glass artists. He was already working with paperweights in the forties. He died early in 1992. In the mid-seventies, Rick Ayotte, Chris Buzzini, Ken Rosenfeld, Victor Trabucco, Debbie Tarsitano and her father Delmo came on the scene. Since the eighties began, Randall Grubb, Gordon Smith, Johne Parsley, Jon and David Trabucco (Victor Trabucco's sons) and Bobbie Banford, Bob Banford's wife, have gained success. Only recently has Paul Stankard's former assistant, Jim Donofrio, become known as an independent paperweight artist.

Blaschka glass flowers, a model for many American glass artists.

Roland ("Rick") Ayotte

Rick first specialized in the realm of bird portrayals in paperweights. As a good friend of Paul Stankard, he could not immediately show the collectors flower motifs similar to Stankard's own. But no one had previously shown birds in paperweights. They are formed so authentically that collectors often cannot tell genuine feathers from those portrayed in glass.

Rick Ayotte has another specialty. Here he does not prepare small three-dimensional pieces to be enclosed, but actually paints with hot colored glass on the hot glass block. He calls these *GlassScapes* (from landscapes).

Since the beginning of the eighties, Rick Ayotte has also shown large, complicated flower and fruit bouquets that fill the whole paperweight. As his birds are known for their realistic feathers, his bouquets are especially fascinating for their detailed reproduction of leaf and fruit surfaces. His paperweights with colorful large butterflies are rarities and very limited in numbers.

All paperweights made by Rick Ayotte are comparatively large (more than 8 centimeters in diameter) but relatively flat. Miniature paperweights (about five cm in diameter) exist in small numbers with only a few motifs. The bases of his paperweights are always polished, ground hollow, and have a hand-engraved signature running around the lower edge of the paperweight outside the base. The maximum number of pieces made with a single motif is 25 to 75. Rarely, though, does he make more than thirty to forty pieces per motif. Rick Ayotte is full of new ideas; it often happens that he suddenly stops long before the end of a planned series and begins to make completely new motifs. All of his paperweights are signed with a handwritten "Rick Ayotte", "R. Ayotte" or simply "Ayotte". The numbers that collectors alone usually want are often missing. He would rather not number his paperweights at all, since they are all genuinely unique works.

Blossoms and buds by Roland Ayotte.

Ray and Bob Banford

The glass industry is traditionally very widespread in New Jersey, the home of the Banford father and son, and since 1985 also of Bobbie Banford. Both men had very early contact with older glass-blowers from Europe whose families had settled in the region around Millville and Vineland about a hundred years ago and still make their homes there.

The Banfords have specialized in (almost) reproductions of the old French paperweights. Viewing the rare old paperweights in the Corning Museum of Glass inspired Ray Banford to take this course. After Charles Kaziun, the Banfords were the first to make paperweights by using the glass-blower's lamp. Their flowers, salamanders and snakes in clear crystal or on colored backgrounds, with filigree or croze backgrounds, with garlands, or millefiori canes, show a height of perfection not attained for a long time. The Banford excellence is emphasized by the many complicated cuts that are not seen in as great variety from any other paperweight artist. This is the unmistakable signature of Ed Poore, probably the world's greatest glass-cutter. In this occupation too, one needs not only a sharp eye and a steady hand but also endless patience. Ed Poore has them all.

The Banfords were also pioneers in the realm of overlay paperweights produced exclusively on the glass-blower's lamp. Yellow, red, blue and dark green double overlays on white have been made by them since 1980.

Only since the end of the eighties has Bobbie Banford, Bob Banford's wife, broken from the classic Banford style with her underwater portrayals. She has gained these new ideas from her experience in underwater diving.

Ray signs his paperweights with a round letter cane of a black "B" in white glass. Bob uses the letter "B" in black with a blue rim. Paperweights are also in existence that were made by father and son together. These works have both signatures. Older paperweights can have different color combinations in the signature canes.

Ray Banford has been retired for the past few years. He still makes a few pieces with his old motifs, particularly his iris flowers in various colors. Since there is a greater demand for these motifs among collectors than Ray can or will meet today, it can be assumed that his son Bob has meanwhile gained complete mastery of these iris blossoms. Thus newcomers to collecting may also be able to acquire these unique iris flowers, so characteristic of Banford work.

Paperweight by Bob Banford.

Christopher ("Chris") Buzzini

Chris Buzzini probably has the most interesting career of any paperweight artist before him. Before he set up as an independent artist in 1986, he was already well-known. He worked first at Orient & Flume, then at the Lundberg Studio, and still later at Correia Art Glass, all in California. Thus he had already mastered the third kind of paperweight production, painting, modeling in hot liquid glass, before he took up lampwork. This experience gave him such a sure hand that he can produce his lampwork paperweights in excellent detail, error-free and to perfection. To this day Chris Buzzini produces single flowers and complicated flower bouquets, always on a clear background. His paperweights are seldom cut. Only the base is cut concave and polished.

He is the only artist who signs his works with his full name "Buzzini," and the date using a white cane. This can be seen clearly only under the best light and only with a loupe. In addition, he engraves his name and the date in handwriting on the side near the base.

Paperweight by Chris Buzzini.

Jim Donofrio

Only in 1991 did this glass artist become known to Amnerica's paperweight collectors under his own name. Many of his products, though, were already known to many, for he had worked as an assistant to Paul Stankard from 1981 to 1986. He probably created the small naked figures in the Stankard paperweights.

The scenes portrayed in Jim Donofrio's paperweights are based on life in the deserts of Mexico and New Mexico. Cactus plants and flowers, bare boulders and desert sand dominate the scene. Dried plants, shards of clay and jewelry of the Amerindian culture lie scattered in the paperweights. They are desert still-lifes. In addition, he models small animals, such as crabs, frogs and salamanders in his paperweights. Some of his paperweights can be told from Stankard's works only with difficulty; the two artists worked so closely for so long.

Jim Donofrio signs his works on the lower side edge with his full name, the year and the ledger number.

John Gooderham

John Gooderham (pronounced "Good-rum") is Canadian. He sells his paper-weights almost exclusively to American collectors. All of his paperweights are extremely small, well under the usual dimensions of four to five centimeters for miniature paperweights, measuring only one to three cm in diameter. John Gooderham generally melts small Italian millefiori canes and gold-foil pressings into his works. His specialty consists of buttons and stickpins, all of which are produced in the same manner as the paperweights. Many of his miniatures are also seen in valuable old doll houses, such as the large doll-house collection at the Chicago Art Institute, as scale models of paperweights and doorstops.

Doll-house paperweights by John Gooderham, diameter 8 to 18 mm.

Randall ("Randy") Grubb

Lavender-colored dahlia by Randall Grubb.

Randy's paperweights are extraordinarily accurate. The motif is always centered, clear and accurate, in the middle of the ball. For some ten years the motifs were flowers that were modeled not necessarily from nature, but freely in form and color. The flower bouquets are rare on colored backgrounds, but usually on clear, colorless ones.

Since 1990, detailed portrayals of grapevines and tendrils of different types of grapes have been Randy's specialty. Like the Banfords, Randy has also mastered the overlay technique. Red, green, blue and mauve double overlays, generally cut with seven windows, give the paperweights an air of elegance.

The paperweights made by Randy Grubb are particularly large, high, and thus almost perfectly spherical, never flat. Until 1991 he signed them with his engraved name and date. Since 1991-92 he has also used a "G" signature cane.

Harold Hacker, Robert and Ronald Hansen

Harold Hacker died in 1989, Ronald Hansen earlier, in 1986. Robert, his brother, has been retired for some years. A son of Ronald Hansen, likewise named Ronald, could well appear as his father's heir to the art of paperweight making.

Harold Hacker specialized in relatively small paperweights (medium size, somewhat larger than miniatures). As well as small flowers and fruits, he specialized in small snakes, salamanders and all other kinds of small reptiles. Depending on the quality of his works, he signed them with his full name or with various abbreviations.

The works of the Hansen brothers, when signed or identified with a white "H" signet cane, include a few very good and valuable creations plus many second-class paperweights. At that time the works of paperweight artists were not judged as critically as they are today. Everything was just in a state of development. The Hansens made their paperweights in their spare time after work. The numbers they made are not known, and all their pieces went to the trade for little money.

Fruits, single flowers and bouquets, and small animals are known. The arrangements often lie on a colored background, and many have been given a window cut later.

These paperweights were not produced in significant numbers, since collecting of these works of art only began to expand in the eighties.

Charles Kaziun

Before, during and immediately after World War II as of 1945, Charles Kaziun experimented with the rediscovery of the old and forgotten paperweight techniques. As a technical glass-blower, he possessed the very best prerequisites for his quest.

Kaziun's works, almost exclusively miniature paperweights (and many even smaller), stand out for their vast variety. He mastered and showed all paperweight techniques. In the smallest space, his works contain snakes, lizards and flowers in the finest lampwork, plus the finest millefiori and filigree sections. Everything always lies on a gentle, colored background of filigree, colored croze and/or gold tinsel. Charles Kaziun also used glittering aventurine glass and drew out his own silhouette canes.

Along with the classic miniature paperweights, which are often signed either by a "K" in a small cane in his older works or later with a very small "K" of gold foil, Charles Kaziun took great pleasure in producing small, even extremely small, perfume bottles. His phials show the same motifs in their bases and stoppers as his paperweights. The stopper often shows the motif standing on its side. Many of his paperweights are melted onto a decorative base. The "Millville Rose" design appears again and again in various colors.

In many paperweights, more or less as a sign of authenticity, a tiny bumblebee or butterfly of gold foil has been melted in for decoration.

The miniaturization of all his work culminates in the so-called paperweight buttons and actual doll-house paperweights that only reveal their beauty and complexity under the loupe. Prior to his death in 1992, these works were made by him and his son Charles Kaziun II, who has followed in his father's footsteps and is now producing paperweights.

James and Nontas Kontes

James and Nontas Kontes, very successful self-made men and owners of a large factory for the production of glass apparatus, were inspired by paperweight collecting to take up the art of paperweight making.

Since the beginning of the seventies they have collected, and since the end of the seventies they have produced their own paperweights after working hours in their own factory.

Their works hardly ever appear on the open market any more, for they find it hard to part with their own creations. From time to time they allow one of their creations to be auctioned off for a worthy cause within the framework of important events, or they trade their works with other glass artists.

In their repertoire, they have mastered flowers, fruits, animals, and large bouquets on a filigree background and/or colored glass. All of their works are unique. They sign them individually, with a "NK" or "JK" monogram, although they make all their paperweights together.

The Kontes brothers' factory has been the training ground for many other paperweight artists who have gone on to achieve success. Among others, their employees have included Bob Banford, Gordon Smith, and until his retirement also Johne Parsley.

Dominick Labino

Only in retirement did Dominick Labrino experiment with glass-blowing. He died in 1987. In terms of the nature of his very small paperweight production, Dominick Labrino should really be classified under the heading of glass studios.

His works as a paperweight artist served as models for the artists who work with liquid kiln glass in the present-day studios.

His works are not preformed, but only shaped in and out of the liquid glass. His paperweights feature garlands of flowers, tendrils on or under the surface, and the motif of the so-called combing technique as well as Marbrie (or marble-) weights with their marbleized outside surfaces. Metal salts in the glass mixture provide shimmering metallic effects. His few paperweights are signed with his name and the year engraved on the base.

Johne Parsley and Gordon Smith

Until about ten years ago, both of these men—Johne shortly before retiring and Gordon as a beginner—worked at the Kontes brothers' glass factory in New Jersey. Along with the Kontes brothers, they became interested in paperweights. At first it was only a hobby for them; now they are successful paperweight producers. At first they helped each other; now each of them has his own studio.

Johne Parsley's works feature exclusively his very small, very detailed flowers. At first there were only tiny red roses in small miniature paperweights that were often cut with windows. A cut bottom star and often an intense cobalt blue as a background are Johne Parsley's identifying marks. Most recently, though, his paperweights have been made larger. But the flowers, including many yellow and black violets, still remain very characteristically small and delicate. His "P" signet can often be seen when one looks in from above.

Gordon usually offers solitary flowers on stalks with leaves and buds on a clear, dark or light blue or dark green background. His realistic representations of orchids are renowned. Gordon is a sport diver, and since the end of 1986 he has also exhibited complicated, bright-colored underwater scenes in his relatively flat and only seldom cut paperweights.

All of his paperweights are engraved with "GES" and the year on the side.

Three raspberries by Gordon Smith.

Ken Rosenfeld

Much like Chris Buzzini, Ken Rosenfeld spent a short time in a glass studio before he became an independent paperweight producer as of about 1980. He also went into practice as a technical glass-blower.

Ken Rosenfeld is known for his great variety of fruit arrangements. Every type of fruit and vegetable has been portrayed by him in paperweights. Squash, carrots, beets, corn, peppers, tomatoes, apples, pears, berries—all can be found in Ken Rosenfeld's paperweights.

His flower and plant arrangements are always a blaze of colors. Unlike the fruits, his flowers emerge, in terms of shape and color, predominantly from the world of his imagination. They are only distantly related to natural flowers. And this is perhaps the particular charm of Ken Rosenfeld's creations for many paperweight collectors: an array of flowers not to be seen in nature in this form.

His paperweights are never cut, but large, somewhat flattened and circular. Rosenfeld often uses, in addition to clear uncolored and transparent tinted glass, a milky opal-white background that is not seen among the works of other paperweight artists.

His paperweights are signed with an "R" glass cane. He also engraves his name and the date on the base.

Garden vegetables by Ken Rosenfeld.

Orange-colored paperweight by Barry Sautner.

Barry Sautner

For the sake of completeness, the works of Barry Sautner should be mentioned here, although they are not paperweights in the true sense and certainly not lampwork paperweights. But the work of Barry Sautner is so rich in imagination that it must not be forgotten here. His works can be compared only to the Diatreta glasses of the Romans.

Barry Sautner has his (raw) paperweights modeled by well-known studio-glass artists with one or more layers of colored overlay. He finishes these paperweights in his studio, making them into his own works of art with a very small sandblaster.

Like the ancient Roman glass artists, who spent months and even years of work with the most delicate tools to work the most delicate structures and forms out of the glass, Barry Sautner spends days and weeks of work with the finest flexible sandblasting equipment to work the shapes he creates, pictorial motifs and miniature sculptures, out of the layers of colored-glass overlay and into the glass. Even three-dimensional multi-colored blossoms can be modeled out of the depths of the glass, hanging or standing only on the thinnest glass stems at the end. His objects are extremely fragile.

The works of Barry Sautner can be compared with the miniatures of the cameo-carvers. All of his sculptures are signed on the base with his full name.

Paul Joseph Stankard

For more than thirty years Paul Stankard has worked with the medium of glass, and for twenty years he has created paperweights of it.

His paperweights feature exclusively flowers, complete plants from the roots to the twigs, leaves and blossoms with their individual parts. Paul Stankard is also an enthusiastic amateur botanist who dissects the plants into all their individual parts before he recreates them accurately in glass and melts them into clear optical crystal glass.

Besides his large, colorful flower bouquets, his complete orchids from his beginning years are renowned. Also famous are his many nude figures who live on the roots in the ground under the plants and apparently take good care of them. He calls them spirits: the very souls of the plants. At the same time, about 1986, there also appeared in Stankard's paperweights the "Orbs", dozens of little "dough-balls" on the roots. This shows the free artistic exposition of Paul Stankard in his paperweights.

For all his works he writes appropriate poetry. He has had his greatest success with his big glass blocks, weighing one to two kilograms, which he developed in 1982 and calls Botanicals. Here Paul Stankard succeeds in portraying complete plants, even as large as life, in a highly decorative manner. Nowadays these glass objects cost several thousand dollars, and their value grows steadily.

Paul's paperweights were the first modern examples of any kinds that appeared at art auctions along with antiques and immediately brought high prices.

Paul Stankard places a small "S" cane into his works. In his older works (from his beginning years to about 1980) it was a "PS". They are also engraved with his name, the date, and a ledger number on the side of the base.

True to life from the roots and earth to the leaves and flowers: Unique work by Paul Joseph Stankard.

Delmo and Debbie Tarsitano

This father and daughter were both so creative and talented that they created the most beautiful paperweights in lampwork. Delmo Tarsitano's specialty was realistic fruit paperweights. He was just as well known for his superb salamanders and snakes in paperweights and the natural-looking scenes around them. Debbie's outstanding works show stylized flowering branches and large flower arrangements in splendid color. These paperweights, often perfectly cut by Ed Poore, reflect the wonderful splendor of colors and flowers.

As collectors of old paperweights, the Tarsitano family had exactly the right feeling for excellent glass. Only since 1978 have Delmo and Debbie Tarsitano sold a portion of their works, which they originally made only for themselves.

Today, after her father's passing in the autumn of 1991, Debbie Tarsitano continues to work in her now-traditional style. Her paperweights already became famous at the beginning of the eighties, when she created a series of engraved paperweights in collaboration with the renowned glass engraver of German ancestry, Max Erlacher of Corning, New York. Here the flowers in the foreground harmoniously wreathe the motifs engraved in the ground by Max Erlacher.

Each paperweight is absolutely unique. A silhouette cane with the monogram "DT", very small and often hidden, is used.

Victor Trabucco and Sons Jon and David Trabucco

Victor Trabucco has been working with glass for almost twenty years. After a brief career as a glass sculptor, he turned to paperweights in 1977. His works stand out through their particular expertise. Characteristic of him are large solitaire roses in pink, red, yellow and dark lilac. Except when colored red, all his flowers show a sheen resembling mother-of-pearl on the flower petals, an invention of Victor Trabucco's. For years he was the only artist who could achieve this effect. For a short time now, the Banfords have also shown this interesting color effect in some of their paperweights.

Victor Trabucco remains unequaled in another technique: He is the only artist who has yet been able to eliminate the formation of so-called crystallization lines and stripes in clear crystal glass. No such borderlines can be found in his works. The blossoms really seem to be swaying freely on all sides in a clear airless space.

Victor Trabucco also made a name for himself with his magnum paperweights measuring more than twelve centimeters in diameter. He portrayed big green lizards, as was previously done only in the old French Pantin paperweights.

His twin sons and helpers for years emulate him today in attaining perfection. They create more strongly stylized bouquets of flowers in all colors. The sizes of their paperweights are smaller than their father's.

Victor Trabucco signs his works with a "VT" glass cane, and also engraves his signature and the date on the lower side of the paperweight. Jon and David have a "T" cane and sign their works with the name of Trabucco. Their paperweights cannot be told apart.

Mayauel Ward

Since 1989, Mayauel Ward has devoted himself to the production of paperweights in addition to working as a glass-blower in a studio glassworks.

In the first two years, he produced only a few miniature paperweights. His two dealers in America and one in Germany always received only three or four pieces from him at long intervals. His ideas for his favorite motifs are generally taken from plant life in the desert sand of his Indian homeland. Beige, lilac, pink, brown, yellow and light blue are his favorite colors, which he uses in flowers, stones and sand.

He signs his paperweights on the base with his full name. Unlike all other paperweight artists, Mayauel Ward cuts and polishes his paperweights himself. In the glass studio in which he usually works, though, he has no complicated glass-cutting machines at his disposal. The identifying mark of his paperweights is that the base is not cut hollow, but only flat. The customary base rim of paperweights is thus not present.

Francis Whittemore

Like many older American paperweight artists, Francis Whittemore began to produce paperweights long before his new and great success, which dates from about 1975.

He made his first simple paperweights as early as 1968, following old French models. His main subject was flowers of all types, and at that time they were still strongly stylized. The individual flowers almost always lie on a transparent colored ground.

Meanwhile Francis Whittemore has halted production. It is very difficult to find paperweights made by him at all, since they were never made in great quantities, to say nothing of being exported.

The "W" glass cane on the base marks all original Whittemore paperweights.

Hints for Collectors

The number of paperweights on the market seems almost infinite today. This applies more to new pieces than to old ones, of course. Specimens from the second half of the past century (from 1845 on) can be regarded as old paperweights.

These are primarily the classic crystal paperweights from France. Here the collector has a wide range of sulphide, millefiori and lampwork paperweights to choose from. The number of cuts on the paperweights is high. Their sizes and versions vary greatly. Their condition extends from very good, almost perfect, to very bad. Depending on their damage, the better cutting possibilities of today make repairs possible, and such repairs can be worthwhile. But such repairs are not always carried out in the right manner.

The prices of these old French paperweights fluctuate on the basis of many different criteria, from a few hundred to several thousand dollars. The situation is much the same as applies to old paperweights from Britain, Murano, Bohemia and the USA. All are found only rarely, especially in Germany. The greatest numbers of them were produced in the USA, in New England. These are also the specimens which can be confused most easily with pieces made in France.

Genuine old specimens from Murano scarcely exist at all. Now and then a millefiori smelling-salts bottle from Murano appears. Genuine paperweights from Bohemia are also extremely rare. Serious misidentifications of them are possible only rarely, as there are great differences in their patterns, colors, glass, specific gravity and workmanship. The paperweights from the various sources scarcely harmonize with each other visually; on the contrary, they look downright strange and different from each other. The mixups that can occur with French and American paperweights (the emigrated glassmakers having come from the well-known French glasworks) normally cannot result in any great financial damage, since the two have attained similarly high prices by now. Extremely expensive examples, with prices in the thousands of dollars, are extremely rare and were made almost exclusively at Clichy and Pantin. The prices of the big rose paperweights made by Mount Washington Glass in America have now risen to $30,000+ and continue to rise.

Great care and skepticism must be applied to the new Murano paperweights as compared to their old French pendants. As long as the prices asked for them are in the area of only a few hundred dollars, not much can go wrong. At several thousand dollars, though, one must exercise caution. With a guaranteed right to return the piece, though, there seems to be no need to have doubts in most cases.

In the period from the turn of the century to about 1960, no particularly valuable paperweights were produced. This does not mean, though, that among the so-called friggers such examples cannot be found that are made very expertly and beautifully. The many butterflies made of colored glass canes may be cited here as an example. But their prices do not yet reach the heights of their professionally made, classic siblings. The collector certainly can find these paperweights, and the choice is almost unlimited.

It must be mentioned at this point that these particular paperweights are being made for commercial purposes today in even greater numbers than in the glassworks during the past eighty years.

The new paperweights from the crystal works, glass studios and individual artists are almost all cataloged from the start, and all are signed and identified. The dealer can provide the buyer with exact data. Price guides exist. The prices of new paperweights and objects similar to them can reach several thousands of dollars today (i.e. Paul Stankard's Botanicals). Higher standards in terms of the quality of the glass, the workmanship and condition can be set today.

In all, many more new paperweights have been created as there are old ones in existence. In spite of that, the numbers of them on the market remain small. The number of collectors has increased tremendously in the last ten years. Despite the greater numbers produced, the rarity of the paperweight is maintained. Only a few kinds of paperweights can be expanded by individual makers into mass production. Not ranking among these are the paperweights, especially those from France and America, that are made individually with the greatest care. These masterpieces of glass art are created by renowned glass artists in many hours or days of handwork.

It would not be a good idea to start collecting paperweights on St. Mark's Square in Venice. Venice is a dream; for the paperweight collector, though, Venice can become a trauma. Nor should one go to China, for Chinese paperweights will be offered to you in the discount houses for ridiculously low prices. Antique dealers also offer them, but not for ridiculously low prices.

The European collector should plan a trip to the United States and visit the museums, the large and small collections. "Photograph" the specimens with your eyes, and a sketch pad. You can spend countless hours admiring the creative powers of glass-blowers in bygone days, and of the young glass artists of today. Don't miss the Art Institute in Chicago. This institute houses in its famous art museum the biggest and most beautiful paperweight collection in the world, the Arthur Rubloff collection. And don't neglect to visit the Corning Museum of Glass on your way to Niagara Falls. Buy yourself more literature on the subject, and later perhaps a videotape on the manufacturing of paperweights too.

In the beginning, buy only from well-known, long-established and "reachable" dealers. When you buy at auctions, don't do it blindly. You need to have held the pieces in your own hand. The best description is worthless if important information is passed over, or if the auctioneer has "made a mistake" or been unclear or only seemed to mean what you thought. If he really made a mistake, and if the business is a reliable one, then there is a possibility of returning the item for a refund.

Always keep in mind that when an item is sold "at a bargain price", it is almost always the seller who gets the best of the bargain. The purchase of an expensive, high-quality paperweight from a specialist with many years of experience, even when the price seems high to you at the moment, will prove to be the better buy in the long run. This paperweight will always retain its value. If you look only for the highest quality, then you will have to realize that the pickings are very slim and the prices very high.

Paul Hollister, a New Yorker known as a paperweight expert and the author of many books about paperweights, wrote about paperweights and the collecting of these "jewels in the collector's crown" twenty years ago: "Paperweights in good, untouched condition are becoming increasingly hard to find, and they are consequently more valuable." (From "Glass Paperweights of the New York Historical Society")

The Care of Paperweights

Do not let paperweights bump against each other. Glass is not elastic; it breaks off, or more commonly, the small impact makes moon- or half-moon-shaped cracks in the depths of the glass.

Never hold and observe paperweights directly above other paperweights. A paperweight can slide out of the hand all too easily. Never hold paperweights in wet or greasy hands. Hold a paperweight, when it is necessary to do so, so that you can grip it with three fingers, the thumb, index and middle fingers, and then immediately put the ring and little fingers under the paperweight. Only thus can it not slip out of your hand. You should practice this grip so that it becomes automatic. A collector learns to take every glass or other costly object into his hands in such a way.

Do not expose paperweights to great changes in temperature. Never wash them in warm or ice-cold water. Paperweights feel best at room temperature. Warning: there are said to be people who wash any glass object in the dishwasher. For paperweights, this is guaranteed to lead to cracks and scratches—if you are lucky. Many of them will break into two or more pieces. Simply wipe paperweights with a damp piece of leather once in awhile. Be very careful to keep them warm if you have to transport them outside in winter. Do not place paperweights in sunlight or in an area that is reached by rays of sunshine! Be particularly careful about the winter sun that shines in at an angle. The burning-glass effect could scorch the surfaces under or near them, or even set fire to them.

Glossary

Air Bubbles
Deliberately made air-bubble inclusions, or larger, unwanted and disturbing air bubbles in the glass.

Air Ring
A circular inclusion of air running around the piece, an air bubble, usually close to the base of a paperweight, often under, over or even in a concentrically turned spiral (see Mercury).

Aventurine
Glass with glittering metal tinsel inclusions; gold aventurine contains metallic copper, green aventurine chrome tinsel, resulting from the partial reduction of the corresponding metallic salts in the colored glass.

"B"
The signature of Baccarat; rare in old paperweights, but always in new crystal goods from this factory.

Basket
a) Nearly semicircular millefiori and/or turned filigree canes running downward enclose a millefiori or lampwork motif like a basket; seen especially in Clichy and Paul Ysart paperweights.
b) A true-to-life reproduction of a small basket made of crystal glass and filled with flowers or fruit.

Bouquet
A flower motif that includes more than one flower; the glass flowers are shaped on the glass-blower's lamp; they can be flat or stand upright, making a three-dimensional bouquet.

"C"
The signature cane in extremely rare Clichy paperweights.

Cameo
Another word for any kind of sulphide inclusions; French "sulfure", German "Porzellan-Pasten-Medaillon".

Canes
Any kind of fine colored glass rods result from repeated melting, repeated dividing and bundling, plus drawing out of the thick colored glass bundle into very thin rods; all the pieces show the same motif in cross-section; it would be incorrect to call them "tubes", since all canes that look like tubes only appear to be tubes. The empty space that appears to the untrained eye to be present in and around the canes is always filled with clear glass.

Carpet ground
Regular, even millefiori ground that looks like a carpet.

Colored glass
Glass colored by the addition of metal oxides to the glass batch.

Crown
Hollow blown paperweight decorated all around with cane ribbon.

Date cane
See Millefiori and Silhouette canes.

Dump
A paperweight or doorstop with air-bubble inclusions, made of green bottle glass in northeastern England.

Filigree
White and/or colored glass fibers that were melted into staffs of clear colorless glass and given spiral, braid or netlike patterns by twisting the rod while still fluid.

Frigger
Paperweights that were once actually made at the end of a work day or during breaks, when broken bits of glass and millefiori canes were melted into a small number of paperweights at random.

Lampwork
Glass work made on a "glass-blower's lamp", formerly burning petroleum, now always an industrial burner.

Macédoine
<A paperweight chiefly containing pieces of colored filigree rods, presorted as a colorful mixed pattern (at Baccarat), or left unsorted.

Magnum
A paperweight with a diameter greater than 8 cm.

Mercury-Mercurius
A mistaken and confusing term, meaning bright air bubbles and rings that reflect like quicksilver in paperweights.

Millefiori
Italian for "thousand flowers". The main motif of paperweights made out of colored canes; their arrangement looks like a carpet of flowers.

Miniature
A paperweight with a diameter smaller than 5 cm.

Overlay
A colored layer of glass that is melted over the glass object, whether drinking glass or paperweight. If multiple layers are applied, it is called double or triple overlay. The special feature of this technique is that the different colored layers set each other off through the subsequent cutting.

"P"
"P" stands for Perthshire Glass, Scotland. This signature cane does not mark the old Pantin paperweights. Pantin paperweights are only known to exist unmarked.

Pastry mold canes
Pieces of colorful millefiori canes, canes that resemble candy canes.

Pontil

A heavy, massive metal rod some 1.4 to 1.8 meters long, with which the glass is taken out of the melting oven and rolled, shaped, held and transported in the various phases of the manufacturing process. A hollow pontil is the so-called glassmaker's blowpipe. With it, the glass-blower can produce hollow articles of glass, such as crown paperweights.

Pontil Mark

The breaking-off point (from the pontil) at the base of all hand-shaped and mouth-blown glasses, including paperweights, almost always removed by cutting and polishing the base surface.

Signature cane

Usually an opaque white millefiori cane showing the paperweight maker's name or initials.

Silhouette cane

An opaque millefiori cane depicting an animal, flower or figure in silhouette.

"SL"

This is the signature of the crystal works at Saint-Louis, France, seen very rarely in old paperweights but almost always in new ones.

Star cut

A star is cut into the bases of many paperweights.

Sulphide

See Cameo.

Super-magnum

A paperweight with a diameter greater than 20 cm, such as the super-magnum piédouche from Saint-Louis.

Torsade

Columns of glass rods of varying colors, sometimes twisted in a rope design.

Window cut

The most frequently used cut for paperweights, with large or small "ball" cuts into the wall of the weight, through which the motif becomes visible as if through a window; it is always needed in overlay paperweights.

Museums with Paperweight Collections

There are many paperweights in museums in the USA today, where they can be seen regularly.

To plan a visit to the Museum für Kunsthandwerk in Frankfurt, one should apply in writing or by telephone and ask about the paperweights that form a special part of the Pfoh-Stiftung. The paperweights in its glass collection are seldom displayed.

This advice also applies to a planned visit to the new Buchheim-Museum in Feldafing.

The Art Institute of Chicago, Chicago, Illinois
  Arthur Rubloff collection
Bergstrom Art Center and Museum, Neenah, Wisconsin
  Evangeline Bergstrom collection
The Corning Museum of Glass, Corning, New York
  Amory Houghton collection
Flint Institute of Arts, Flint, Michigan
Glynn Vivian Art Gallery, Swansea, Wales, Great Britain
Henry Ford Museum, Dearborn, Michigan
Illinois State Museum, Springfield, Illinois
  Morton Barker collection
Musée du Verre, Liege, Belgium
New York Historical Society, New York City
  Jennie Sinclair collection
St. Mary's Seminary, Perryville, Missouri
  Estelle Doheny collection
Sandwich Historical Society Museum, Sandwich, Massachusetts
Smithsonian Institution, American History Dept., Washington D.C.
Wheaton Museum of Glass, Wheaton Village, Millville, New Jersey
Buchheim Museum, Feldafing, Bavaria, Germany
  (write for appointment)
Museum für Kunsthandwerk, C. & M. Pfoh-Stiftung, Frankfurt am Main, Germany

Photo Credits

Many collectors who remain anonymous, the Paperweight Club of Germany at P.O. Box 1733, 8033 Planegg, Germany, and the firm of Farfalla-Paperweights in Starnberg have supplied all of the photographic material and information for this book, for which the authors and the publishers thank them heartily.

Bibliography

The Art Institute of Chicago, Glass Paperweights, *USA, 1991.*

Capote, Truman, Wenn die Hunde bellen/Die weisse Rose, *novel, Munich.*

Casper, Geraldine J., Glass Paperweights of the Bergstrom-Mahler Museum, *USA, 1989.*

Cloak, Evelyn Campbell, Glass Paperweights of the Bergstrom Art Center, *USA, 1969.*

Elville, E. M., Paperweights and other Glass Curiosities, *England, 1954.*

Farfalla, Paperweights-Fotomappe, *Munich-Starnberg, 1976-1993.*

Hollister, Paul, The Encyclopedia of Glass Paperweights, *USA, 1969.*

———, *and Lanmon, Dwight P., Flo*wers which clothe the Meadows, *USA, 1978.*

———, *Gla*ss Paperweights of the New York Historical Society, *USA, 1974.*

Imbert, R, and Amic, Y., Les Presse-papier Français de cristal, *France, 1948.*

*Ingold, Gérard, Pa*perweights aus Saint-Louis, *Munich, 1986.*

———, *Saint-Louis, Fro*m Glass to Crystal, *Paris, 1986.*

Jokelson, Paul, One Hundred of the Most Important Paperweights, *London, 1966.*

———, *Sulp*hides, *USA, 1968.*

Kulles, George N., Identifying Antique Paperweights Millefiori, *USA, 1985.*

———, *Ide*ntifying Antique Paperweights Lampwork, *USA, 1987.*

McCawley, Patricia, Antique Glass Paperweights from France, *England, 1968.*

———, *Gla*ss Paperweights, *England, 1975.*

Mackay, James, Paperweights—Briefbeschwerer aus Glas, *Munich, 1980.*

Malpass, Eric, Morgens um sieben ist die Welt noch in Ordnung *novel, Reinbek, 1967.*

Manheim, Frank J., A Garland of Weights, *USA, 1967.*

Mannoni, Edith, Sulfures et boules presse-papier, *France, 1983.*

Newman, Harold, An Illustrated Dictionary of Glass, *London, 1977.*

PCA: Bulletins of the American Paperweight Club, *USA, 1953-1993.*

PCD: Bulletins of the German Paperweight Club, *Munich, 1980-1993.*

Sarpellon, Giovanni, Miniature di Vetro, *Venice, 1990.*

Selman, L., and Pope-Selman, L., Paperweights for Collectors, *USA, 1975.*

Sotheby's, Concise Encyclopedia of Glass, *London, 1991.*

Stankard, Paul J., The First Decade, *USA, 1979.*

Tait, Hugh, Five Thousand Years of Glass, *London, 1991.*

Wodehouse, P. G., The Purloined Paperweight, *novel, USA, 1967.*

Ysart et al., Ysart Glass, *England, 1990.*

Paperweight Illustrations

About the Illustrations and the Price Guide

The paperweights illustrated in the following section provide a good overview of the variety of paperweights made by various manufacturers and artists from the earliest years, the middle of the past century, and the modern day, that have been offered for sale at auctions and in the trade. The condition of the pieces is perfect as a rule; any damage is noted in the captions. They certainly affect the market value but are unavoidable in the extremely sensitive material and cannot always be restored. For the serious collector, damaged paperweights nevertheless offer the opportunity to possibly obtain a rare, long-sought piece at a relatively modest price in order to complete and round off his collection.

In the price guide the sometimes considerable differences between similar paperweights will attract attention. This is, for one thing, a result of particular signs of quality that generally remain unseen by the layman, and also of the particular rarity of a special specimen that is perhaps only in existence as an individual piece and thus very sought-after. In special cases, prices may be charged that go far above the listed sums.

Let us say a few words on the subject of damage to paperweights. A type of repair or restorative work, very popular in the USA, is the complete recutting and polishing of the entire paperweight. In the process, of course, the paperweight always becomes smaller, and also flatter on its upper curvature. After such restoration, the base also appears to be brand new. Such a recutting is particularly disadvantageous if inner motifs are no longer located in the center, or if the areas near the rim disappear from sight or become obscured.

During such work, tension cracks can even appear that are first exposed by recutting after more than a hundred years.

Particular care and caution should be exercised when the paperweights show a flat cut or various types of faceting cuts that may possibly indicate that there might have been major damage, a place where the glass was struck or spintered. Here the collector must decide for himself whether he will have a chance to find a specimen in original condition, or whether he—for an appropriately low price—should buy the repaired specimen.

It may be surprising that it is not always the age of a paperweight that determines its market value. Thus the prices of paperweights that are considerably newer, such as those from Pantin, bring much higher prices than older ones from Baccarat, Clichy and Saint-Louis. In addition to the rarity of individual specimens, the optical beauty, the enchantment, and the perfection that has been attained in a piece often plays a role in determining its value. In the same way, works of a modern glass artist, such as those of Paul Joseph Stankard, often equal and even exceed the values of old paperweights.

The values quoted in the catalog should be regarded by buyers and sellers alike as guides which depend, like the value of other goods, on the powers of supply and demand.

One more bit of advice based on experience: As a serious collector, never buy a paperweight just because it seems to be a bargain to you. Your pleasure will not last long. It is not the quantity, but the quality of the specimens and the harmony of the collection, that makes an impression. A high-quality, high-value paperweight, even though it seems expensive to you when you buy it, will always retain and even increase its value. A profusion of pieces, on the other hand, makes them look cheap. And consider that in paperweights you have your choice among thousands, in beautiful paperweights, among hundreds, and in superb pieces, among dozens. So always buy only the example that pleases you best. The saying of an old collector friend will give you something to think about:

"Collect carefully, collect only quality—quantity soon causes space problems."

Bohemia
1845-1855

1 Spaced Millefiori
Colorful millefiori with silhouette canes on white filigree.
Diameter 6.9 cm

2 Double Overlay
Red and white overlay, concentric millefiori red and white on white filigree.
Diameter 7.1 cm

3 Spaced Millefiori
Colorful millefiori, individual silhouette canes and two devils, butterfly on white filigree.
Diameter 6.8 cm

4 Concentric Millefiori
Red-white-green and white-red millefiori on white filigree.
Diameter 7 cm

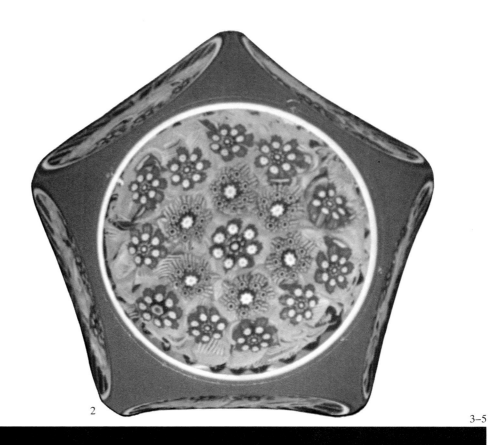

2

3–5

1

5 Patterned Millefiori
Very rare. 16 pink Clichy roses alternating with 8 white canes in outer wreath, and a wreath of blue canes around a white middle cane. Base is concave. Glass darkened afterward by effects of light.
Height 3.3 cm, diameter 5.5 cm

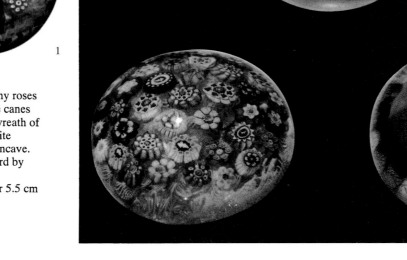

1-5 $610-2440

Murano
Italian, circa 1845

Characteristics: comparatively dark "gloomy" colors and glittering gold aventurine inclusions.
Pietro Bigaglia exhibited the first millefiori paperweights at the Industrial Exposition in Vienna in 1845.

1 Scrambled
Dated and signed "POB", 1845, with silhouette canes (animals and gondolas).
Diameter 7.2 cm

2 Scrambled
Dated 1846, many silhouette canes (animals, gondolas, man).
Diameter 7.7 cm

3 Scrambled
with animal silhouette canes, undated.
Diameter 7.5 cm

4 Phial
with silhouette canes.

Depending on the number, variety and beauty of the silhouette-canes and whether with or without a date:
1-4 $610-3050

1

1–3

4

Antique French Paperweights
Mid-19th century

1 Saint-Louis, White Pompom Dahlia with Bud
Pink colored grid ground.
Diameter 7.0 cm $6100

2 Baccarat; Patterned Millefiori
Red and green circles; arrow-rod cane in the center, arranged around a turquoise and white millefiori wreath. Very rare motif.
Diameter 7.9 cm $9150

3 Clichy; Barber's Pole or Checker Weight
Pink and pistachio green Clichy rose and colorful millefiori canes between blue and white twisted filigree.
Diameter 7.6 cm $6100

4 Saint-Louis; Carpet Ground
Apricot-color with silhouette canes: dancer, devil, horse, camel and dog. Very rare motif; one of the "one hundred of the most important paperweights" listed by Paul Jokelson.
Diameter 7.1 cm $10,650

5 Saint-Louis; Millefiori Mushroom
Colorful millefiori, blue-white torsade, star cut on the base.
Diameter 7.7 cm $7925

6 Clichy; Swirl or Spiral
Dark blue and white, white cane in the center.
Diameter 8.5 cm $3050

7 Saint-Louis; Crown Paperweight
Colorful torsades alternating with white twisted filigree. Parerweight is hollow.
Diameter 5.6 cm $2750

8 Baccarat; White Double Clematis with Bud
Arrow-rod cane in center, star cut on base.
Diameter 6.4 cm $2750

9 Saint-Louis; Scrambled or Frigger
Colorful millefiori cane sections mixed together haphazardly.
Diameter 7.8 cm $725

10 Clichy; Flower on Filigree
Wreath of pink and light green millefiori canes.
Diameter 6.6 cm $4875

11 Baccarat; White Double Clematis with Bud
"Star honeycomb cane" surrounded by a wreath of red and white millefiori canes, star cut on base.
Diameter 7.2 cm $3950

12 Saint-Louis; Concentric Millefiori
Colorful millefiori laid in concentric circles.
Diameter 8.0 cm $2440

13 Saint-Louis; Crown Paperweight
White twisted filigree, alternating with green-white-red torsades. This paperweight is hollow.
Diameter 8.3 cm $8225

14 Clichy; Clichy Rose Garlands
Made of colorful millefiori canes and 12 white and green Clichy roses, one rose and pistachio green Clichy rose in the center.
Diameter 7.6 cm $6400

15 Saint-Louis; Pelargony or Cornflower
on white grid ground, bright blue flower petals with ochre-yellow midpoint.
Diameter 6.5 cm $5800

16 Clichy; Scattered Millefiori
on turquoise blue background, colorful millefiori and a rose and pistachio green Clichy rose.
Diameter 6.1 cm $2750

17 Baccarat—Strawberries
Red fruits and green leaves, star cut on the base.
Diameter 7.0 cm $7310

Baccarat

Antique Millefiori Paperweights from 1848

Close Millefiori
Mid-19th century, signed and dated, with silhouette canes. Possible dates: 1846 (rare), 1847, 1848 and 1849 — sometimes also with letter "B". Every date consists of four or five white canes together. The numbers are in color combinations with red, blue or green. In this type of paperweight there is a great variety of silhouette canes, such as the rooster, dog, horse, elephant, goat, black ape, white ape, devil, squirrel, lovebirds, pelican, swan, pheasant, stork, dove, butterfly, clover leaves and various flowers.
Diameter 4 to 10 cm
$1825-6100

Values are determined by the size of the paperweight, number and types of silhouette canes, presence or absence of date, perfection of pattern and general condition.

Baccarat, Saint-Louis and Clichy, Miniature Paperweights

circa 1850, undated

1 Baccarat; White Double Clematis
with two buds, star cut on base.
Diameter 5.3 cm $3050

2 Clichy; Spaced Millefiori
with a pink and pistachio green Clichy rose.
Diameter 5.5 cm $1220

3 Saint-Louis; Frigger or Scrambled
with a silhouette cane.
Diameter 5.3 cm $1220

4 Baccarat; Pompom Dahlia
Apricot-colored, star cut on the base.
Diameter 4.5 cm $2130

5 Clichy; Spaced Concentric Millefiori
on filigree, with white and pistachio green, white and pink, pink and pistachio green Clichy roses.
Diameter 5.2 cm $1525

6 Clichy; Patterned Millefiori
with ten pink and pistachio green Clichy roses.
Diameter 4.8 cm $1220

7 Baccarat; Red Double Clematis
with millefiori garlands, star cut on base.
Diameter 5.5 cm $1825

8 Clichy; Flower
with one white Clichy rose.
Diameter 6.2 cm $1525

9 Baccarat; Concentric Millefiori
Pink and white canes.
Diameter 5.2 cm $610

10 Clichy; Spaced Millefiori
with one white and pink and one pink and pistachio green Clichy rose.
Diameter 5.3 cm $915

11 Saint-Louis; Crown Weight
with 20 torsades, very rare color combination.
Diameter 5.3 cm $2750

12 Saint-Louis; Patterned Millefiori
with millefiori garlands.
Diameter 5.3 cm $300

13 Clichy—Flower
with three colorful flower canes and five green leaves.
Diameter 4.3 cm $1035

14 Baccarat—Pansies
Star canes in the center, star cut on the base.
Diameter 5.3 cm $915

15 Clichy; Concentric
One rose and pistachio green Clichy rose in the center.
Diameter 4.5 cm $610

16 Baccarat—Primrose
Royal blue with white rim.
Diameter 5.5 cm $1340

17 Clichy—Swirl
Blue and white, green cane in the center.
Diameter 4.7 cm $2130

18 Clichy; Patterned Millefiori
with eight pink and pistachio green Clichy roses.
Diameter 4.4 cm $915

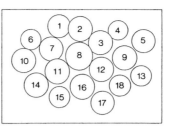

Baccarat
Mid-19th Century

Baccarat; Flower Weight
Red and white primrose, pink dogrose with white rim of flowers and leaves, red double clematis on white filigree with millefiori garland and red double clematis with millefiori garland on clear ground. Diameter 6 to 7.5 cm
$1525-2130

Baccarat
Mid-19th Century

Baccarat and Saint-Louis Flower Weights
The blue double clematis by Baccarat (lower left) and Saint-Louis (center) differ clearly in their center canes: a complex millefiori cane in the Baccarat and a yellow match-head cane in the Saint-Louis piece, a millefiori garland around the flowers in the Baccarat.
Diameter 6.5 to 7.5 cm
$2440-5500

Baccarat

Mid-19th Century

Pansy Weights
of the three French crystal
works, Baccarat (lower right),
Clichy (center and upper right),
and Saint-Louis (upper and
lower left).
The most varied versions are
found in the Saint-Louis
pansies.
Diameter 5.5 to 7.5 cm
Baccarat $1220-1825
Saint-Louis $1825-2440
Clichy $2440-4270

Clichy

Mid-19th Century

**Clichy Millefiori Paper-
weights**
regularly and irregularly laid
out—with the typical Clichy
roses in pink, white, green and
turquoise. The outer row of
canes—which occurs in the
most varied colors, is drawn out
toward the bottom, much
resembling a basket and thus
also called a millefiori basket
weight.
Diameter 6.6 cm $2440-3660

Clichy Magnum "Basket Weight"

circa 1850

Basket of white vertical bands of glass with red and white torsades at the upper and lower rims. In the green moss ground are fifteen millefiori groups in cobalt blue, coral red, yellow, purple, apricot, red and white, including seven white Clichy roses. In addition, 25 pink Clichy roses are included in the millefiori pattern. This basket weight is the only known example of this type from Clichy and very certainly also the most outstanding Clichy paperweight. It is believed that this basket was originally made complete with a handle.
Height 6.5 cm, diameter 10.9 cm
(Sold by Sotheby's, New York, in 1990 for $258,500)

Saint-Louis and Clichy

circa 1850

Flower-Garland Weights

Small flowers (posies) lie on white filigree (typical of Clichy—the canes of glass fiber are carefully arranged side by side at the lowest level). The "garland weight" with the six pink Clichy roses is unique. Left and center: Clichy; right: Saint-Louis

Diameter 6.4 and 7.4 cm

$4875-7320

Saint-Louis

Mid-19th Century

Three Saint-Louis Paper-weights
made of lead crystal, "wreaths" and "strewn flowers".
The special feature of this type of Saint-Louis paperweights is the unusually simple form with a very sparse motif.
Different techniques: lampwork leaves and flowers with mille-fiori centers or lampwork leaves combined with millefiori flowers. Sometimes star cut on the base.
Diameter 7.5-8.5 cm
$1825-3050

Saint-Louis

circa 1850

"Pompom Dahlias"
on colored grid ground. White dahlias on pink grid and pink dahlias on white grid.
The pompom dahlia motif was first made by Saint-Louis. The different type of flower prep-aration suggests different periods of manufacture.
Diameter 6-7 cm $3660-7310

Sulphide Paperweights

circa 1850

1 Baccarat "Rock Weight with Portrait Sulphide"
A white cameo with an extremely rare portrayal of a man's two-sided head—the second, identical portrait lies facing down to the bottom— over a glittering green-sprinkled aventurine sand ground.
Diameter 7.5 cm $1525

2 Baccarat "Hunter with Dog" Sulphide
White cameo on transparent green ground, facet cuts all around.
Diameter 8.5 cm $2440

3 "Napoleon" Sulfide Weight, Saint-Louis
Sulphide portrait with the inscription "L. Napoleon" on a clear ground with a wreath of blue and red millefiori canes.
Diameter 7.9 cm $725

1

2

4 Baccarat "Bouquet" Sulphide
White sulphide—pansies held
by two hands—on a clear
ground.
Diameter 6.7 cm $610

5 Baccarat "Queen Victoriä Sulphide
White portrait sulphide on
transparent cobalt-blue ground.
Diameter 8 cm $2130

6 Baccarat "Joan of Arc" Sulphide
White cameo on red transparent
ground, facet cuts all around.
Diameter 8.5 cm $2440

Medallions melted into glass objects first appeared in Britain and France toward the end of the 18th century. It was preceded by the development of the porcelain-paste medallion by Wedgwood and Sevres.

These decorations became particularly widespread in very thick-walled cut drinking glasses and crystal tumblers. Later, around the middle of the 19th century, a great many of them, especially portrait medallions, were melted into paperweights as well.

The following terms have been used for this popular type of glass incrustations: Sulphides, sulfurs, crystallo ceramic or ceramie, cameos, cameo incrustations, porcelain-paste and glass-paste medallions, crystal ceramics, Kameen and Kameen-Einschmelzungen.

3

4

5

6

1–4

Pantin
Middle to End of the 19th Century

Very realistically portrayed roses, fruits (strawberries, cherries, pears, etc.) and salamanders are ascribed to the Pantin crystal works in France.

1 White Rose
with many green leaves and red ground.
Diameter 6.7 cm

2 Yellow Rose with Bud
and green leaves on white opaque ground.
Diameter 7.6 cm

3 Red Rose with Bud
and blue-green leaves on white opaque ground.
Diameter 7.6 cm

4 White Lilies of the Valley
with two dark green leaves on a clear ground.
Diameter 7 cm

5 Red Currants
A branch with red and unripe green currants on a stem with green leaves, clear background.
Diameter 7.8 cm

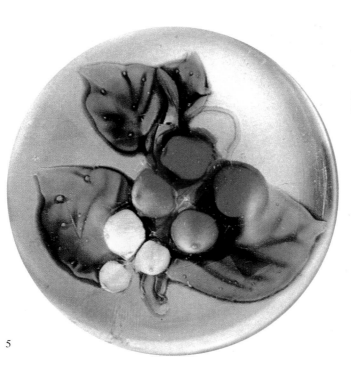

5

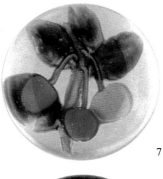

7

8

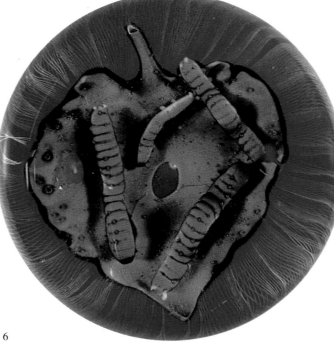

6

6 Silkworms
Four flesh-colored caterpillars on a green mulberry leaf with holes, white filigree over a bright blue ground.
Sold by Sotheby's of New York, December 1983.
Diameter 9.2 cm

7 Cherries
Three red cherries hang on a twig with four green leaves, clear ground.
Diameter 5.5 cm

8 Strawberries
Two red berries and one green one with three green leaves, clear ground.
Diameter 6.2 cm

Lilies of the Valley
and Fruits: $3050-4875
Rose Paperweights: $4875-9150

Bacchus Paperweights

circa 1850 (1848-1855)

Concentric Millefiori
in light pastel colors, not signed or dated.
Diameter ca. 9 cm $610-1825

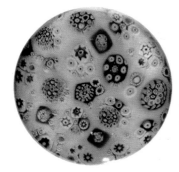

Mount Washington Glass Company

circa 1859

1 Mount Washington Magnum Rose
Pink rose with two buds and green leaves, on a clear ground.
Diameter 11 cm $38,415

2 Mount Washington Magnum Rose
Apricot-colored rose with two buds and green leaves, on a clear ground.
Diameter 10.5 cm $27,440

3 Mount Washington Magnum Rose
Blue and white rose with one yellow and one white bud and green leaves on a clear ground.
Diameter 10.5 cm $27,440

4 Mount Washington Magnum Strawberries
Symmetrically arranged red strawberries and white blossoms on a clear ground.
Diameter 10.5 cm $18,290

5 Mount Washington Magnum Rose with Butterflies
A filled red rose with two buds and a colorful butterfly on each side, typical of Mount Washington work.
Diameter 10 cm $27,440

1

Sandwich (Boston & Sandwich Glass Company)

1850 to 1880

The paperweights made by Sandwich and by the New England Glass Company (NEGC) are often very hard to identify, since some of the glassmakers worked for both companies; for example, Nicholas Lutz worked for two years for NEGC, then for Sandwich, and afterward for the Mount Washington Glass Company.

1 Pansy
Light blue and white flower with white "Clichy rose" in the center, clear ground.
Diameter 7.7 cm

This type of paperweight has been ascribed to the Frenchman Nicholas Lutz (born 1835 in Saint-Louis, France). From 1869 to 1888 he worked as a glass-blower for Sandwich. This also explains the similarity to the Saint-Louis pansy weights.

2 Clematis
Around a yellow central cane lie six pink petals—with glittering gold and yellow dots—and six pink-striped white petals, clear ground.
Diameter 7.5 cm

2

1

3 Clematis
Arranged around a white central cane are twelve blue-striped white petals, clear ground.
Diameter 7.5 cm

4 Clematis
Arranged around a yellow central cane are six light blue petals with yellow dots and six white petals with blue dots, clear ground.
Diameter 7.7 cm

1-4 $1220-1825

3

4

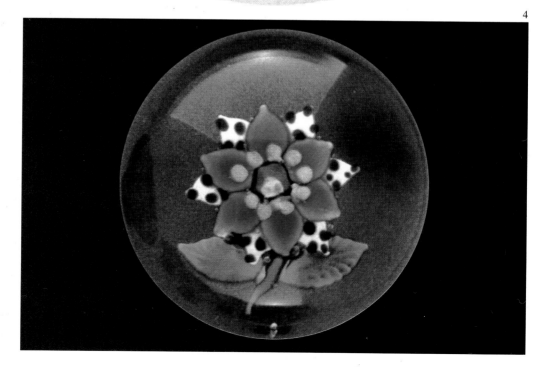

New England Glass Company (NEGC)

Mid-19th Century

1 Red Clematis
with green leaves on white filigree ground.
Diameter 7.7 cm

2 Bouquet
Flowers in yellow, blue, lilac, red, orange and white on a white filigree ground.
Diameter 7.7 cm

3 Flower
with millefiori garlands on filigree ground.
Diameter 6.6 cm

4 Fruits
and green leaves on a filigree ground.
Diameter 7 cm

5 Patterned Millefiori
on white filigree ground.
Diameter 7 cm

6 Basket of Roses
Red and white roses in a green plaited basket on a white filigree ground.
Diameter 5 cm

1-6 $915-2130

2

3–6

"Bohemian" Paperweights

Beginning of the 20th century

1 & 2 Crown Weights
Made of colorful twisted glass rods that are brought together into a common central point and resemble a crown—often in several stages. (Probably from Stryia, circa 1900).

3 Stylized Flower
made of red and white glass rods and arranged over a colorful croze ground.

4, 5, 6 Sulphide Paperweights
"Squirrel", "Lion" and "Hand with Marguerite" daisy on colorful croze ground. Motifs made of porcelain material; the same motifs are often found since molds were prepared and these figures were cast in large quantities, but not exclusively for use in paperweights.

7 Ornamental Paperweight
cut in so-called combing technique with "spun" red and white glass filaments.
Diameter 7 to 9 cm
1-7 $185-365

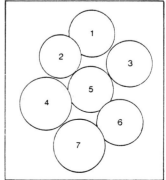

"Bohemian" Paperweights

Beginning of the 20th century

Flower Paperweights

Flowers made partly by lampwork technique, usually with a white or colorful speckled pillow. Often these paperweights were also decorated with multiple cuts.
Diameter 7 to 9 cm $122-300

This type of paperweight was made not only in Bohemia or elsewhere in Czechoslovakia, but also in Thuringia (including Weisswasser), in the Bavarian Forest and in Austria.

The glass is often tinted light green, brown or bluish, or has been darkened by sunlight over the years.

The assortment of patterns is infinite. One can find two similar specimens that come from the same glassworks, made by the same hands, but one will never be able to find two fully identical "Bohemian" paperweights from this period.

"Bohemian" Paperweights

Beginning of the 20th century

Paperweights with Names, Initials and Inscriptions

"Oskar 1912", "H.S.", "P.R." and "Emil" come from the Weisswasser area in Thuringia. "H.K."—these letters were made of copper wire and laid in—"F.S.G." and "Zum Geburtstag" (for your birthday) were written with liquid glass directly on the glowing glass core during the manufacturing process; and "Wilh. Förster Lehrer" and "Gruss aus Thüringen" (Greetings from Thuringia) were first written on an opaque white glass plate in cold technique and the plate was then inserted.
Diameter 6 to 9 cm $122-300

Millefiori Paperweights from Thuringia

Beginning of the 20th century

Colorful Millefiori
on a pillow of colorful glass croze.
Diameter 5.5 to 8 cm
$122-185

China

circa 1930

1 Blue Butterfly
With blue marguerite daisies on an opaque white ground.*
Diameter 6.5 cm

2 Red Bird of Paradise
on opaque white ground.*
Diameter 5.6 cm

3 Pansies
on a white grid ground (Imitation of the antique French pansy paperweights).
Diameter 7.1 cm

4 Millefiori
in green, white and red. The cane in the center is blue and white. Very flat paperweight.
Height 3.3 cm, diameter 6.5 cm

5 Millefiori
in white, red, blue and green. Very flat paperweight.
Height 2.3 cm, diameter 6 cm

1-5 $60-300

* The motif was painted on the white glass plate (cold technique) and then covered with glowing liquid glass.

China

circa 1920-1930

Flower basket
White basket made of glass filaments with a handle of white and pink torsade, filled with small millefiori flowers in orange-red, light blue, dark blue and green, each with a yellow "matchhead" center.
Diameter 8 cm   Individual piece, $610

1

2 + 3

4 + 6

The typical colors that dominate Chinese paperweights are orange, yellow, red, green and white; they make identification very easy. The base almost always has a relatively small, irregular, matte, smooth-cut (but not polished) surface.

China— Modern Paperweights

post-1960

1 Large white flower
with red stripes laid on and two white butterflies.
Diameter 8.5 cm

2 Four White Crocuses
with yellow stamens and green leaves.
Diameter 7.3 cm

3 White Flower
with yellow stamens and green leaves that are arranged on several levels.

4 White Cockatoo
in a green opened blossom with many petals; paperweight with a small stand.
Height 7.5 cm, diameter 6 cm

5

5 Branch with Flowers
with orange flowers and white egg-shaped leaflets.
Height 9.3 cm, diameter 8.5 cm

6 Orange Opened Blossom
with yellow flower stem; paperweight with small standard.
Height 8.1 cm, diameter 7 cm

1-6 $30-90

1 **Macédoine**
2 **Concentric Millefiori**
3 **Garlands on Filigree**
4 **White Carpet Ground with Signs of the Zodiac**
5 **Close Millefiori with Signs of the Zodiac**
6 **Spaced Millefiori on Filigree**

Millefiori paperweights of lead crystal; colorful canes arranged in various patterns. Signature "B" millefiori cane and date. Firm's trade mark also etched and year, serial number and quantity (for example, 1980 50/200) engraved on the base. Diameter 8 cm

1-6 **$300-915**

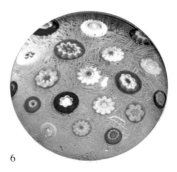

6

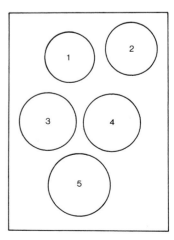

Baccarat

1971 to 1979

Gridel Paperweights

Every paperweight shows all 18 motifs in small silhouettes, differently arranged. In each case one of these silhouettes is also found in the center in a larger size, and this determines the name of the piece. Millefiori technique. White signature cane with black letter "B" for Baccarat and year, i.e, B 1971. The Baccarat firm's trade mark is also etched and the year and serial number of the paper-weight are engraved on the base.

Year	Motif	Quantity
1971	Rooster	1200
1972	Squirrel (71)	1200
1973	Elephant (74)	400
1973	Horse	400
1974	Pelican	400
1974	Swan	400
1974	Hunter	400
1975	Black Ape	400
1975	Turtle Dove	400
1975	Pheasant	400

Year	Motif	Quantity
1976	Stag	400
1976	White Ape	400
1977	Red Devil	400
1977	Stork	400
1978	Dog	400
1978	Goat	400
1979	Butterfly	400

Diameter 7.5 to 8.5 cm

$610-1220

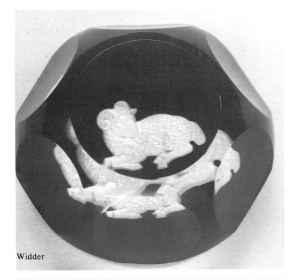

Widder

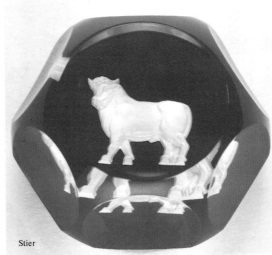

Stier

Löwe

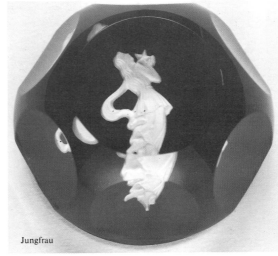

Jungfrau

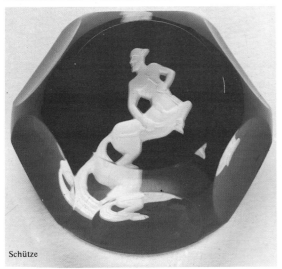

Schütze

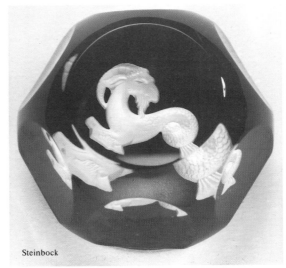

Steinbock

Baccarat

modern

Sulphide Paperweights, "Signs of the Zodiac"
White cameo on royal blue transparent ground. Window cut. Standard 6 mm high.

Signature: Baccarat firm's trade mark etched on the base. Quantity: unlimited, not dated. (Since about 1976)
Diameter 7 cm $245

Saint-Louis

1987

1 Huckleberries
Twig with blue berries and green leaves on a bluish-green ground; two-row ball cut, window cut above.
Diameter 8 cm   Quantity 150. $725

2 Yellow Anemone
White and yellow flower with green leaves on clear ground. An antique paperweight motif served as a model.
Diameter 7.5 cm   Quantity 250. $580

3 Wood Anemone Bouquet
on white filigree. The motif fills the paperweight completely and is overlaid by only a thin layer of crystal glass.
Diameter 7 cm   Quantity 250. $725

4 Double Overlay "Millefiori Mushroom"
Double overlay—yellow and white—surrounding a millefiori mushroom (concentric pattern).
Diameter 8 cm   Quantity 250. $1100

5 Millefiori "Compact"
Colorful millefiori fills the paperweight completely to close below the surface; overlaid only by a very thin layer of crystal glass.
Diameter 8 cm   Quantity 250. $725

Gemini

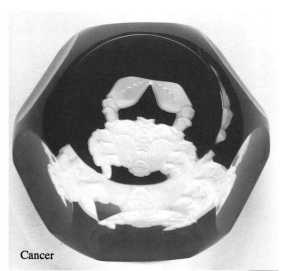

Cancer

Libra

Scorpio

Aquarius

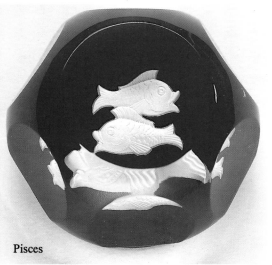

Pisces

6 Enclosed Double Overlay, "Hunting Motif"

A bouquet of flowers standing upright, covered with a double overlay—red and white—with engraved hunting motifs, then encased in clear crystal glass. Encased paperweights rank among the most complicated and riskiest motifs in all paperweight manufacturing. Only the crystal works of Saint-Louis still produces these masterly achievements today, and only in small quantities.
Diameter 10 cm   Quantity 25.
$550

7 Millefiori "Venetian Mosaic"

A modern, new-age pattern made of colorful millefiori canes.
Diameter 7.5 cm   Quantity 150.
$975

8 Millefiori "Alhambrä

The variation on a well-known antique millefiori pattern used in Saint-Louis paperweights.
Diameter 8 cm   Quantity 250.
$1035

9 Perfume bottle "Yellow Crocuses"

Cut phial with cut stopper of clear crystal glass, an arrangement of yellow flowers on the bottom of the bottle.
This phial was made with blue flowers in a strictly limited special issue for the French fashion designer and perfume producer Balmain.
Height 15 cm   Quantity 50.
$610

Illustrations on pages 98, 99.

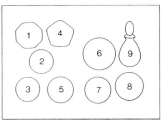

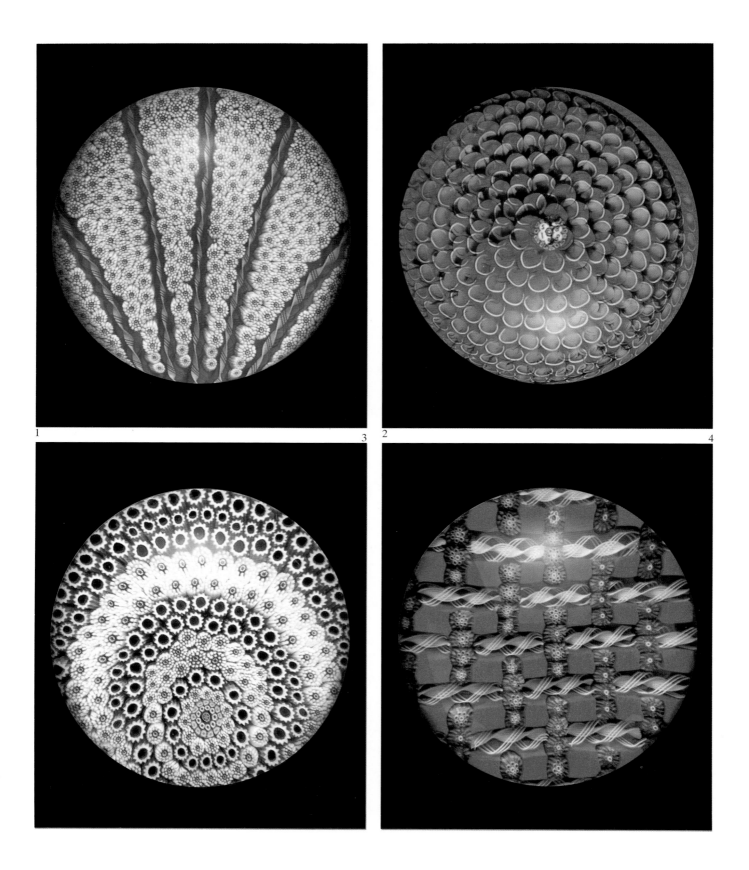

1
3
2
4

Saint-Louis

1988

1 Fontäne
Thick white millefiori divided
by blue and white torsades.
Diameter 7.5 cm   Quantity 400.
$670

2 Harmony
Green millefiori canes laid in
concentric circles, with the
signature cane SL 1988 in the
center.
Diameter 7.5 cm   Quantity 400.
$670

3 Shells
Millefiori pattern of rust-
colored canes and fine white
rods.
Diameter 7.5 cm   Quantity 400.
$670

4 Fondant
Ochre-colored millefiori canes
and white torsades on a green
ground, making a woven
pattern.
Diameter 7.5 cm   Quantity 400.
$670

5 Summer Dream
Colorful millefiori and green
leaves (lampwork) on a red
ground, forming a spiral.
Diameter 7.7 cm   Quantity 400.
$670

6 Heralds of Spring
Colorful flowers with green
leaves on a white opaque
ground (lampwork).
Diameter 8.3 cm   Quantity 200.
$915

**7 The Blue Flower
of Romanticism;
Encased Overlay**
A three-dimensional blue
flower standing upright in a
blue and white encased (coated
with clear crystal) double
overlay.
Diameter 9 cm   Quantity 70.
$3110

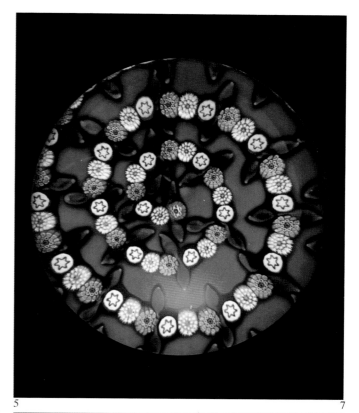

6

5

7

Saint-Louis

1989

1 Rose Garden
Red rose with buds (lampwork)
on a cobalt blue ground,
window cut.
Diameter 8.5 cm   Quantity 300.
$850

2 Harlequin
Colorful millefiori canes
arranged in a star pattern.
Diameter 7.5 cm   Quantity 300.
$850

3 Butterfly
Pistachio green butterfly and
pink flower on a light blue
ground (lampwork).
Diameter 8 cm   Quantity
250. $850

4 Ladybug
Three white flowers with green
leaves and a ladybug on a blue
background (lampwork).
Diameter 8 cm   Quantity 200.
$945

5 Orchid
Pink orchids with bud and green
leaves on an opaque white
ground (lampwork).
Diameter 8 cm   Quantity 250.
$850

6 Robin
Bird on a branch with red
cherries, white ground
(lampwork).
Diameter 8 cm   Quantity
300. $850

7 Gingham; Encased Overlay
A colorful three-dimensional
flower standing upright in a red
and white encased (covered
with clear crystal) double
overlay, with a gingham pattern.
Magnum weight.
Diameter ca. 9.5 cm
Quantity 50. $6100

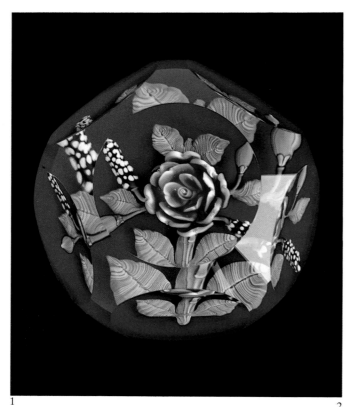

1

2

3

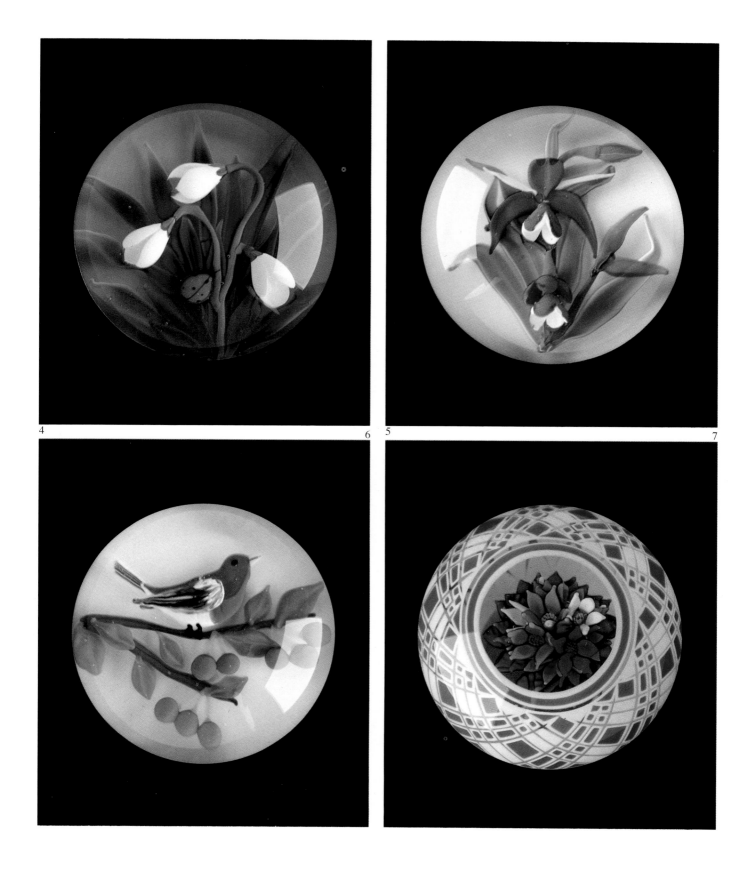

4

6

5

7

Saint-Louis

1990

1 Owl
On light green ground (lampwork).
Diameter 7.5 cm   Quantity 500.
$915

2 Poetry
Flower bouquet with blue and white blossoms on a light green ground.
Diameter 8.2 cm   Quantity 500.
$1100

3 Orchid
Colorful orchids on a white ground.
Diameter 8.2 cm $1100

4 Fioretti
Light blue millefiori canes, white inside and with wavy rims, laid out in concentric circles.
Diameter 7.7 cm $850

5 Persian Pattern
Graphic pattern of red and blue millefiori canes.
Diameter 7.7 cm   Quantity 600.
$1035

◁ 1 + 2   3–5 ▷

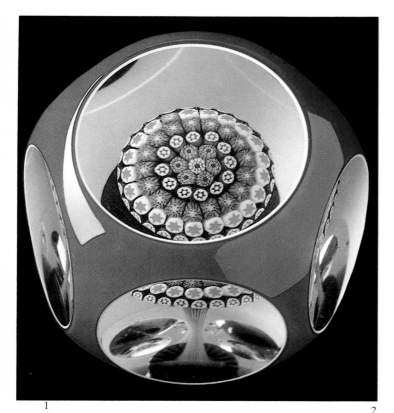

Saint-Louis

1991

1 Artistica
Green and white double overlay with millefiori mushroom and window cut.
Diameter 7.5 cm   Quantity 250.
$1100

2 King
Magnum crown weight with blue-white-red and green-white-red twisted glass rods, alternating with white filigree.
Diameter ca. 9.5 cm
Quantity 150. $2075

3 Artifice
Three-dimensional flower bouquet. Many facets.
Height ca. 10 cm   Quantity 150.
$2135

4 Poet
Patterned millefiori in white, green and red.
Diameter 7.5 cm   Quantity 300.
$975

5 Oriental
Patterned millefiori in red, white and green.
Diameter 8 cm   Quantity 300.
$975

6 Island
White blossoms and green leaves on a green background (lampwork).
Diameter 8 cm   Quantity 250.
$1100

7 Lady
White roses with buds on a blue ground, window cut.
Diameter 8 cm   Quantity 250.
$1100

4–7 ▷

Saint-Louis

1991

Impressionists

1 Renoir, "La Rose".
2 Monet, "L'Iris".
3 Gauguin, "Les Tahitiennes".
4 Van Gogh, "Le Tournesol".

Signed with a millefiori cane "SL 1991" and also numbered on the base.
Diameter ca. 8 cm
Quantity 300. $5100 each

Saint-Louis

1992

1 Tourbillon-Swirl
White and green spirals on a turquoise ground, red Clichy rose in the center.
Diameter ca. 8 cm
Quantity 300. $790

2 Sarah
Red millefiori in concentric circles.
Diameter ca. 8 cm
Quantity 300. $790

Illustrations on pages 110, 111.

Signature cane of the Cristallerie de Saint-Louis

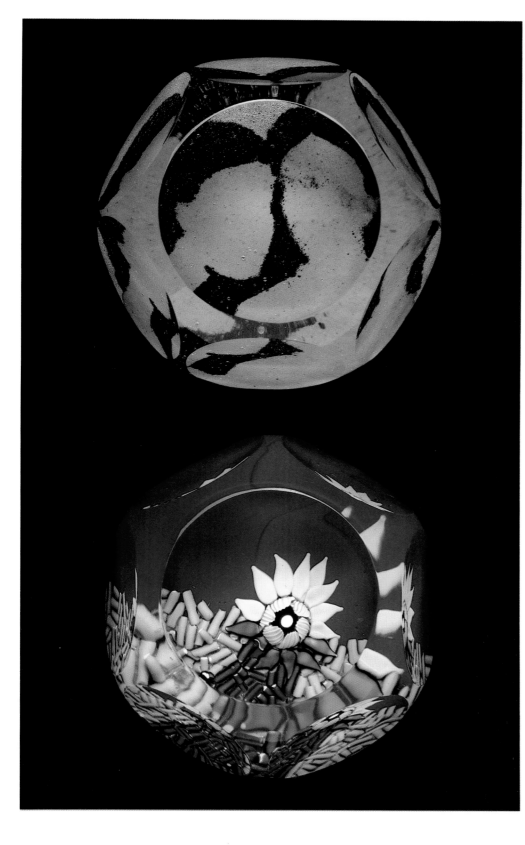

Illustrations on pages 110, 111.

->

3 Piédouche
Basket with white carpet-ground millefiori and multicolored canes.
Diameter 8.5 cm Height ca. 8 cm
Quantity 150. $1700

4 Fascination
Profusion of cherries, honeycomb cut, magnum weight.
Diameter ca. 10 cm
Quantity 150. $1950

5 Viola
Flowers on turquoise blue ground, window cut.
Diameter 8.5 cm
Quantity 250. $1100

6 Corona
Floral wreath on a clear ground, star cut on the base, very flat paperweight.
Diameter 8.3 cm
Quantity 300. $790

7 Veronica
Bouquet of white wild roses on pistachio green ground, window cut.
Diameter 8.5 cm
Quantity 250. $1035

8 Dentelure
Blue and red millefiori garlands on white filigree.
Diameter 8 cm
Quantity 250. $1220

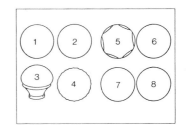

Sulphide Paperweights, Cristallerie de Saint-Louis

Cameos by Gilbert Poillerat, medalist and engraver.

1 General de Gaulle
White cameo with a wreath of white millefiori canes—five of them with the Cross of Lorraine—on a green ground, window cut. Signature: millefiori cane "SL 1976". Diameter ca. 7 cm Quantity 2000.

2 General de Gaulle
White cameo covered with red and white double overlay, window cut. Signature: etched Cross of Lorraine and "SL 1978".
Diameter 8 cm Quantity 700.

3 General Washington
Gold medal of General Washington on horseback, surrounded by 13 white stars (the first 13 states)—one with signature "SL 1976"—on a dark blue ground, window cut. Diameter 7.2 cm Quantity: 1050, 400 of them with red and white double overlay.

4 Statue of Liberty
Pressed gold foil on a dark blue ground, red and white overlay, window cut. Signature: millefiori cane "SL 1986".

5 President Jimmy Carter
White cameo on a dark blue ground, window cut. Signature: millefiori cane "SL 1977". Diameter 8 cm Quantity: 800, 300 of them with red and white double overlay.

1-5 $300-915

1

5

2–4

Murano

Millefiori Paperweights

1 Blue and White Flower
Millefiori discs are laid on the glowing hot glass core and turned so that a flower standing upright is formed (similar to the making of the inserted "Bohemian" flowers). Murano, Italy, 1975.
Diameter 8 cm $30

2 Millefiori
Colorful flower pillow between pink and white torsades, clear ground, dated with a white cane with black number "1885" and a silhouette cane. Manufacturer: Fratelli Toso, Murano, Italy, 1977.
Diameter 8 cm $90

1

2

3 Trees
Made of individual millefiori canes—similar to a mosaic picture. New "Murano millefiori technique" since about 1985.
Diameter 9 cm $90-120

3

Murano

Millefiori Paperweights

1 Blue and White Double Overlay
with millefiori mushroom, made by Fratelli Toso, Murano, Italy, 1977.
Diameter 7 cm

2 Millefiori
Colorful flower pillow between pink and white twisted bands. This motif was also made with the false date of "1885"—a large white cane with black numerals—by Fratelli Toso, Murano, Italy, 1977.
Diameter 8 cm

3 Butterfly
made of millefiori sections over a pillow of air bubbles, by Ferro & Lazzarini, Murano, Italy, 1977.
Diameter 6.5 cm

1-3 $30-120

Whitefriars

Millefiori Paperweights

1 Random
A multitude of various very
fine, colorful millefiori canes,
long window cut. Millefiori
paperweight made of lead
crystal. Signed and dated 1979.
Diameter 7.5 cm $315+

2 Large Owl and Night Sky
Dark ground, window cut.
Whitefriars millefiori paper-
weight made of lead crystal.
Signed and dated 1979.
Diameter 7.5 cm $360+

Whitefriars

Millefiori Paperweights

1 "Farfallä Large Butterfly
Dark ground, window cut.
Millefiori paperweight made of
lead crystal. Signed and dated
1979.
Diameter 7.5 cm $360+

2 Colorful Garland
on a blue ground. Millefiori
paperweight made of lead
crystal. Signed and dated 1977.
Diameter 7.5 cm $300+

1

2

Whitefriars

Millefiori Paperweights

1-4 Butterfly, Fish, Robin and Owl

White middle cane with animal silhouettes of very fine millefiori canes—surrounded by concentric colorful millefiori, window cut. Millefiori paperweight made of lead crystal. Signed and dated, 1977 to 1908.
Diameter 7.5 cm $300+

5 Torsade

Small stone cut, millefiori paperweight made of lead crystal, signed and dated, 1977 to 1980.
Diameter 7.5 cm $260+

6 Torsade, Butterflies

Window cut, millefiori paperweight made of lead crystal, signed and dated, 1977 to 1980.
Diameter 7.5 cm $300+

7 Torsade

Window cut, millefiori paperweight made of lead crystal, signed and dated, 1977 to 1980.
Diameter 7.5 cm $240+

1–4

5–7

Whitefriars

Millefiori Paperweights

1 Scattered Flowers

Colorful millefiori on a transparent turquoise ground, window cut. Millefiori paperweight made of lead crystal. Signed and dated, 1977. Diameter 7.5 cm $240+

2 Flower Bouquet

Colorful millefiori on a transparent blue ground, window cut. Millefiori paperweight made of lead crystal. Signed and dated, 1977. Diameter 7.5 cm $355+

1

2

Whitefriars

*Millefiori Paperweights,
1976 to 1980*

**Millefiori Paperweights
of Lead Crystal**
Various millefiori patterns with
different types of cuts, signed
and dated.
Diameter ca. 8 cm $210-365+

Whitefriars Label, circa 1850
On the underside of a
Whitefriars paperweight (firm
located in London).

Caithness Glass

1 Antennae
750 made, 1983.

2 Fantasia
750 made, 1981.

3 Jester
1000 made, 1981.

4 Loop the Loop
750 made, 1987.

5 Vigil
750 made, 1987.

6 Summer Meadows Butterfly
150 made, 1985.

7 Blue Spray
250 made, 1986.

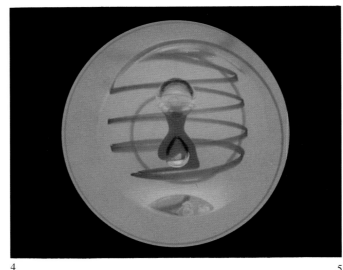

4

7

1

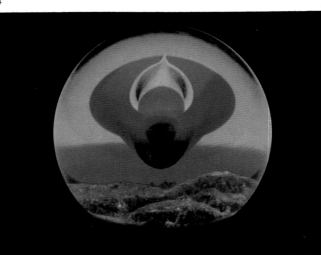

5

2

6

"The Whitefriars Collection", made by Caithness since 1981:

8 Rings of Roses
Unlimited numbers, with 1982 signature cane and the original Whitefriars emblem, the stylized white monk. The original Whitefriars paperweights were produced only until 1980; any years after 1980 indicate that the paperweight was made by Caithness Glass. Diameter 7.5-8.5 cm
$210-550

3

8

John Deacons Christmas Paperweights

O Tannenbaum
Christmas tree with candles and colorful ornaments (lampwork) on white filigree. Quantity 101. Signature: white cane with blue letters "JD", and year "1990" with red, green and blue numbers on the base.
Diameter 7.2 cm $300

Jay Glass Paperweights

1978 and 1979

1 Flowers
Three yellow ocher flowers on a green ground. 101 made, 1978.

2 Blue Dahlia
on white filigree, 101 made, 1979.

3 Yellow Ocher Flower
on transparent red ground. 101 made, 1978.

4 Patterned Millefiori
striped pattern, alternating filigree and millefiori, 101 made, 1979.

5 Colorful Butterfly
on transparent green ground, 101 made, 1979.

6 Christmas Tree
with candles and bright ornaments, filigree ground. 101 made, 1979.

7 Crown Weight
Red and green torsades alternating with white filigree, 101 made, 1979.

8 Wild Roses
on a dark ground, 25 made, 1978.

9 Blue Flower
on blue aventurine ground with millefiori garland, 101 made, 1978.

10 White and Blue Clematis
on clear ground, 101 made, 1979.

11 Blue Dahlia
on white filigree, 101 made, 1979.

12 Flowers
Two flowers on a dark ground, 101 made, 1978.

13 Yellow Ocher Flower
on a transparent red ground, 101 made, 1978.

14 Bouquet
Three flowers (light blue, pink and white, and yellow ocher) on a dark background, 101 made, 1978.

15 Thousand-Petal Rose
on transparent lilac ground, 52 made, 1978.

1-15:
Signature: cane with "J" (1978) and also with year (from 1979 on).
Manufacturing technique: millefiori and lampwork combined.
Diameter 5 cm $185-300

1

2–5

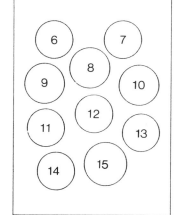

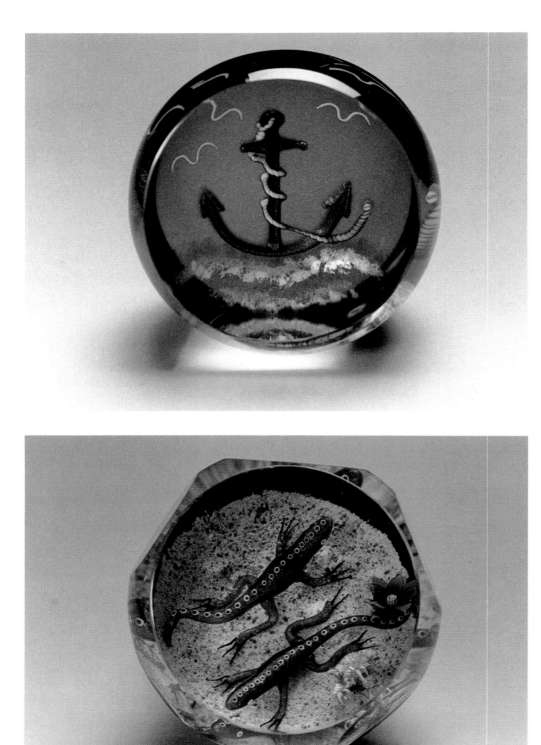

William Manson

1992

1 **Anchor with Ship's Cable**
2 **Salamander Pair**
3 **Flowers with Ladybug and Butterfly**
4 **Octopus**

Base cut smooth, signature cane "WM" and/or engraved on base "William Manson", sometimes with year.
Diameter 8 cm $240-610

William Manson

from 1979 on

The fantastic paperweight world of William Manson shows glittering fish, lizards and salamanders, frogs, dragonflies and birds—often also with flowers as decoration.

Not all signatures are the same. Some of his paperweights made in recent years have a "WM" cane and are also hand-engraved "William Manson", plus the name of the paperweight and the year (or some of this) on the base.
Diameter 7 to 9 cm $300-600

Perthshire Paperweights

from 1979 on

1 Crown Weight
Red and green torsade, alternating with white filigree, a silhouette cane in the center. 300 made, 1985.
Diameter 7.5 cm $365

Patterned Millefiori
on a colored ground, unlimited numbers made.
Diameter 7.5 cm $80

3 Miniature Millefiori
in concentric circles with a colored ground, unlimited numbers made.
Diameter 4 cm $35

4 Pink Clematis—blue and white overlay
Lampwork, 400 made, 1979.
Diameter 5.5 cm $300

5 Golden Dahlia
A multitude of golden yellow flower petals made by lampwork, set at four levels, window cut, 300 made, 1986.
Diameter ca. 8 cm $610

6 Close Millefiori
Colorful millefiori, surrounded by a white torsade, on a transparent blue ground, 300 made, 1983.
Diameter 7.5 cm $230

7 Wreath
Fine lampwork combined with millefiori, on white filigree, window cut, 300 made, 1983.
Diameter 7 cm $260

8 Millefiori
Colorful canes laid in concentric circles on a clear ground, unlimited numbers made.
Diameter 6 cm $75

9 Red Clematis
on a white grid ground, 400 made, 1985.
Diameter 5.7 cm $275

10 Crown Weight
White and gold spirals on a dark blue ground, encased, 300 made, 1984.
Diameter 7.5 cm $425

11 Spring
Small bouquet made by lampwork on a light blue ground, window cut, 250 made, 1982.
Diameter 6.5 cm $455

12 Pink Carpet Ground
with a blue dahlia in the center, 300 made, 1983.
Diameter 7 cm $260

13 Golfer
on a filigree ground with millefiori garland, top cut, 400 made per year.
Diameter 7.5 cm $210

14 Millefiori Sun Wheel
on a colored ground, "P" signature cane, unlimited numbers made.
Diameter 7.5 cm $80
Signature: melted-in cane with latter P.

Jay Glass Paperweights

Scotland, 1978-1979

15 Flower
101 made.

16 Patterned Millefiori
101 made.

17 Wild Rose
25 made.

18 Flower with Bud
101 made.

19 Thousand Petal Rose
52 made.

"J" signature cane and year, blue, red and green on white ground.
Diameter 5.5 cm

15-19: $185-245

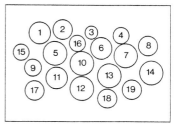

Strathearn Glass

1976

In most cases, the base of the millefiori paperweights is slightly concave with a visible uncut pontil mark. The individual millefiori canes are often very strongly misshapen.

1 Millefiori
Irregular on colored opaque ground.

2 Patterned Millefiori
pressed into a star mold.

3 Millefiori
with blue and white double overlay, signed and dated with one cane, also with serial number and quantity made engraved on the base. 150 made yearly.

4 Flower
Three-dimensional flower standing upright in a cut glass paperweight. Signed and dated.

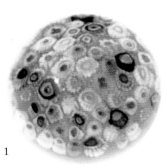

1

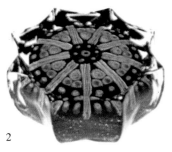

2

4

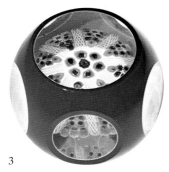

3

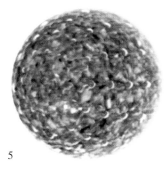

5

5 Aurora
Colorful glass croze decorated
with small inserted air bubbles.
Unlimited numbers made.

Right:
6 Patterned Millefiori
Clear ground, signed and dated
with a cane.

1-6: Diameter 4/6.3/7.5 cm
$30-150

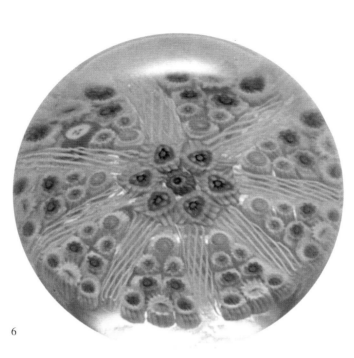

6

Selkirk Glass

1989

Paperweights in contemporary designs:

1 Arctic Lights
2 Spiral Star
3 Scimitar
4 Whispers
5 Filigree
6 Sea Pearl

Signature hand-engraved on the
bottom surface: Selkirk Glass
Scotland, name of the paperweight, serial number and
quantity made, year.
Diameter 7-5 to 8 cm
$60-240

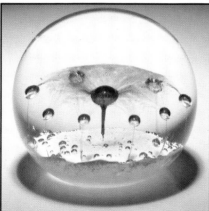

1

2

3

4

5

6

1

2

Peter Holmes
Selkirk Glass

Peter Holmes, while working at Caithness Glass, had the renowned Paul Ysart as his teaching master for traditional paperweight techniques (lampwork, millefiori).

1 Wild Rose
White blossom with red rose hips on a clear ground (lampwork), 75 made, 1982.

2 Millefiori Crown
White twisted glass filaments alternating with red-green-white torsades; one millefiori cane in the center, 150 made, 1982.

3 Primrose
Yellow flowers on a dark ground (lampwork), 200 made, 1981.

4 Filigree Flower
Pansy in a pale lilac glass-filament basket (lampwork), 100 made, 1984.

5 Basket Flower
Clematis, white and lilac blossom in a basket of violet millefiori canes (lampwork), 100 made, 1985.

6 Filigree "Bouquet"
Three flowers in a basket of fine white glass filament, window cut, 100 made, 1985.

7 Basket Flower "Anemone"
White flower with red veining in a blue and white filament basket.
Diameter 7 cm   100 made, 1987.

1-7:
Signature cane with "PH", and "Selkirk Glass Scotland", name of the paperweight, number made and serial number, and year engraved on the bottom surface.
Diameter 7 cm $185-485

3

4

6 5

7

8

9

Peter Holmes
Selkirk Glass

8. Ebony
Black and white tree in contemporary design, 450 made, 1987.
Diameter 7.5 cm

9 Phantom
Contemporary black and white design, 500 made, 1987.
Diameter 7.5 cm

10 Midwinter
Stylized winter landscape, 450 made, 1987.
Diameter 7.5 cm

11 Summertime
Dragonfly with white water lily on blue ground (lampwork). Magnum paperweight with pressed surface and front window cut at an angle, 75 made, 1991.
Diameter 10 cm $455

12 Moonshadow
Black and white lunar landscape with glowing gold air bubble, 500 made, 1987.
Diameter 7.5 cm

13 Sea Mist
Contemporary design, 500 made, 1991.
Diameter 8.5 cm

"PH" signature cane, and hand-engraved "Selkirk Glass, Scotland", name of paperweight, serial number, quantity made, and year, i.e., 1/75 1991.

$150-210

10

11

12

13

Paul Ysart

from 1971 on

From 1963 to 1970 Paul Ysart worked for Caithness Glass and made paperweights in his spare time, before he founded the Paul Ysart Glass Company at Wick in 1971. Simpler paperweights from this period are often signed with an "H" cane.

1 Turquoise Butterfly
Lampwork with millefiori garland on a dark ground.
Diameter 8 cm

2 Millefiori Star
Colorful millefiori on a light blue ground.
Diameter 7.3 cm

3 Patterned Millefiori
Colorful millefiori circles on a dark blue ground. Signed with a "PY" cane.
Diameter 7.2 cm

4 Close Millefiori
Irregularly arranged colorful millefiori.
Diameter 7.3 cm

5 Basket Flower
Red clematis in a basket of millefiori canes (lampwork combined with millefiori).
Diameter 7 cm

6 Butterfly and Flowers
Lampwork, green and blue butterfly with pink flowers, blue and white croze background. Paperweight with a small base. "PY" cane in a flower.
Diameter 8.2 cm

1-6:
Unsigned: $300-610
Signed "PY": $610-1525

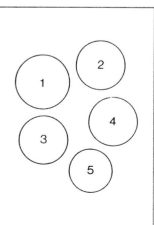

6

Correia Art Glass

*Paperweight Artist Chris
Buzzini—to end of 1986*

Manufacturing technique:
Studio-glass paperweights with
traditional lampwork, matte
opaque outer surface with
angled window polished to a
high gloss. Production: 150,
200 or 250 pieces. Signature:
"Correiä, year made, serial
number and quantity (for
example, 106/200) engraved on
the base.
Diameter 7.5 cm $245-300

1 Colibri
2 Colorful Flower Bouquet
3 Red Bird
4 Blue Bindweed
5 Butterfly
6 Owl with Moon
7 Flamingo
8 Blue Fish
9 Jungle Orchid
10 Pink Flower
11 Dolphin

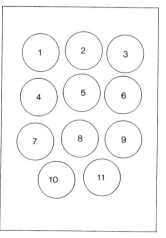

Correia Art Glass

post-1980

1 Paperweight Elite
Sandwich construction: red filaments on clear glass, first overlaid with clear, than aquamarine blue, finally with dark blue glass, matte gold surface, cut sides and highly polished.
Diameter 9 cm

2 Obelisk Elite
Clear glass overlaid with cobalt blue.
Height 12 cm

3 Twilight Orbit
Matte gold surface with highly polished angled window.
Diameter 8.5 cm

4 Obelisk Elite
Clear glass overlaid with aquamarine blue, with silver filaments.
Height 14 cm

5 Sea Gulls
Modern motif in red and silver on dark glass, overlaid with a thin layer of clear glass.
Diameter 6.5 cm

6 Hearts
Red hearts and gold tendrils on iridescent egg-shaped paperweight.
Height 10 cm

7 Triangle
Dark blue glass over aquamarine blue and clear glass, three sides cut and highly polished.
Height 9 cm

8 Paperweight Elite
Sandwich construction: Clear glass first overlaid with aquamarine blue, then with dark blue glass with silver filaments; sides cut and highly polished.
Diameter 9 cm

9 Snake
Blue snake on iridescent gold relief paperweight.
Diameter 7.5 cm

10 Saturn
Dark blue planet with aquamarine blue ring.
Diameter 13 cm

11 Moon and Sea
Iridescent dark blue ring with silver motif, matte surface.
Diameter 6.5 cm

12 Frog
A green frog with green water-lily leaves and black ball, relief paperweight.
Diameter 7.5 cm

1-12:
Quantity made: 125, 200 or 250. Signature hand-engraved on the base. "Correiä, year, serial number and quantity made, i.e., 15/125.
$185-490

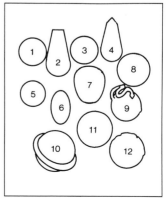

Lotton Studio

Studio-glass Paperweights by Charles Lotton and his Sons David, Daniel and John.

1 "King Tut-Ankh-Amun"
Olive green ground with cobalt blue design (combing technique), matte surface, by Charles Lotton, 1983.

2 "Feather"
White opaque ground with blue decor and gold rim (combing technique), by Charles Lotton, 1983.

3 "Millefiori"
White canes with green leaves (encased), by David Lotton, 1987.

4 "Web"
Iridescent blue, matte surface (combing technique), by David Lotton, 1990.

5 "Leaves"
Gold leaves on a lemon yellow ground, overlaid with a thin layer of clear glass, by Daniel Lotton, 1983.

6 "Pink Flowers"
with olive green leaves in clear glass (encased), by David Lotton, 1991.

7 "Feathers"
Iridescent blue decoration on a Chinese red ground, overlaid by a thin layer of clear glass, by Daniel Lotton, 1984.

8 "Leaf & Vine"
Apricot leaves with black tendrils on several layers, one over another (encased), by John Lotton, 1992.

1-8:
Signature hand-engraved on the base, the name in script—as given here, usually with the date, and sometimes also the name of the paperweight design.
The paperweights made in this studio are not subjected to strict rules as to their size. The same motifs exist with 6.5 cm or 8 cm and even larger diameters.
$90-300

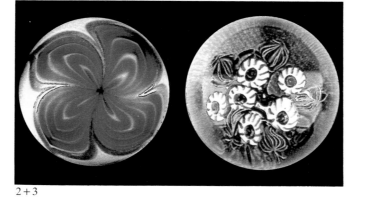

2 + 3

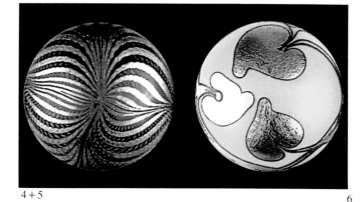

4 + 5

6

7

1

8

Lundberg Studios

post-1975

The first encased paperweights in "California technique" from Lundberg studios, from 1978 on:

1 Orchid
Red lady-slipper on a blue ground.

2 Orchid
Small red lady-slipper on a dark ground.

3 Pink Butterfly
with a pink flower on a light iridescent ground.

4 Light Green Butterfly
with a pink flower on a light iridescent ground.

5 Aquarium
Yellow striped fish between water plants and corals, light iridescent ground.

6 Pink Dahlia
on an iridescent light blue ground.

1-6:
Signature hand-engraved on the base: "Lundberg Studios", year, name of artist and registry number.
Diameter 7 cm $245-300

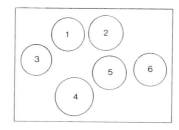

Lundberg Studios

Glass Artists: Steve Lundberg and Daniel Salazar

---

1 Red Azalea Flowers
Clear ground.

2 Wistaria with Butterfly
Light ground.

3 Red Plum Blossom with Butterfly
Blue ground.

4 Lotus Blossoms
White blossoms on a blue ground.

5 Red Phlox Blossoms
White croze ground.

6 White Crane
Blue ground.

7 Dragonfly with White Dogwood
Clear ground.

8 Lilac-colored Daisy
White opaque ground.

9 Fuchsia
Blue ground.

10 Blue Heron with Moon
Blue ground.

11 Veil-tailed Fighting Fish
Underwater landscape, light ground.

12 Fish in Reeds
Clear ground.

13 Red Cherry Blossoms and Butterfly
Light ground.

14 Blue Gentian
Colorful croze ground.

15 Yellow Wild Sundew
Clear ground.

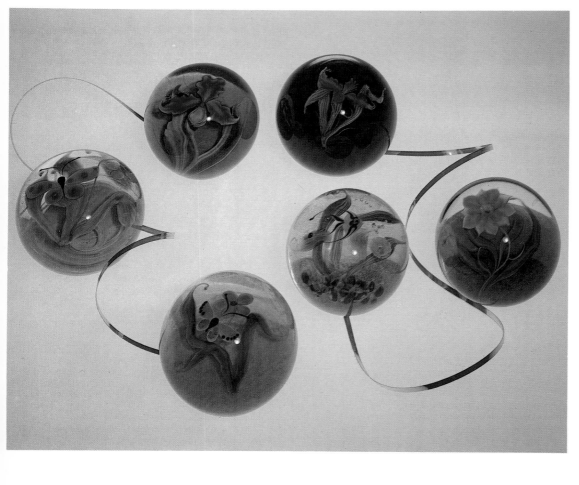

1-15:
Manufactured by the California technique, encased. Quantity made: 250. Signature: hand-engraved on the lower rim: Name of the artist, "Lundberg Studios", year, registry number and quantity made (for example: Steven Lundberg Lundberg Studios 1990 033005 16/250), sometimes also a white cane with blue star and "LS" and the last two digits of the year. Encased paperweights are made in two sizes: Miniature paperweights from 5.5 to 6.5 cm, and the normal size from 7.5 to 8.5 cm.

$300-550

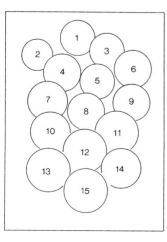

Orient & Flume Glasstudio

post-1975

Iridescent Paperweights:
Hearts, flowers and animals, butterflies, dragonflies and birds—with clear, gold or blue iridescent surfaces. Manufactured by the "California technique".
Signature hand-engraved on the base: "Orient & Flume", registry number and year, for some years also the artist's name, serial number and quantity (for example Alexander 105/250). Quantity made: 250, no limits on some individual motifs.
Diameter ca. 8 cm $210-300

Until about 1985, Orient & Flume had a very varied assortment of graphic motifs with combing technique in its production program, such as geometric forms, feathers, ribbed twist and peacock, and also individual millefiori paperweights (garlands on filigree).

Orient & Flume Glasstudio

post-1985

Encased Paperweights:
Flowers and animals, spiders, butterflies, ducks and peacocks—on colored or clear grounds. Produced by the California technique. Signature: hand-engraved on the base: "Orient & Flume", registry number and year, for some years also artist's name, serial number and quantity made (i.e., Beyer 15/250). Quantity made: 250, no limit on some individual motifs. Diameter ca. 8 cm $300-610

Parabelle Studio

1991

Classic millefiori paperweights, in the style of those made at the French crystal works at Clichy in the past century.

1 Garlands—Pink and Lilac
Patterned millefiori on a green moss ground.

2 Flower with white Clichy Roses
on white filigree with millefiori wreath.

3 Piédouche
Lilac and white basket with colorful millefiori in concentric circles.

4 Carpet Ground
White with individual, very unusual millefiori canes (pansies and Clichy roses). The white carpet ground was made of over 3000 small star canes.

5 Close Millefiori
Colorful millefiori, irregularly located.

6 Pansies
on white filigree with blue millefiori wreath.

7 Flower
on white filigree with a wreath of green and red millefiori canes.

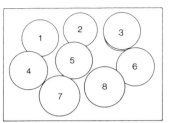

8 Blossom Basket
Complexly made clematis on white filigree in a basket of green and pink canes.

1-8:
Manufacturing technique: drawing of millefiori canes and melting in on a glass oven.
Quantities made: 12, 25 and 75.
Signature: millefiori cane with white, blue-rimmed letters and numbers, with a red-rimmed white bell in the center, for example "PB 1992".
Diameter 7 to 7.5 cm
$300-915

David Salazar

since 1985

David Salazar has been making paperweights in his one-man studio since 1985.

His assortment is varied and includes paperweights in the so-called "California technique" with scenes from the underwater world (sea horses, fish), relief paperweights with flowers and butterflies, and paperweights where the motif extends to just beneath a thin layer of clear glass, i.e., "Marbrie", "Night Sky" or "White Gull".

His specialty is making very small paperweights.

Signature hand-engraved on the base in cursive: "David Salazar" and year.
Diameter 3.5, 5 and 7 cm
$60-300

Josh Simpson

1992

Josh Simpson works at the oven in his studio, making unique contemporary paperweights in various sizes. His subjects are inhabited and uninhabited planets with spectacular landscapes: active volcanoes, blue oceans, thick woods and continents with extensive areas.

Possibly Inhabited Planet
Inhabited Planet
Mega World

Signature hand-engraved on the base: "Simpson" and year.
$185-610

Depending on their size and type, these Simpson paperweights can cost over $18,000 each.

Banford Paperweights

Flower paperweights made by the American artists Ray, Bob and Bobbie Banford

1 White Lady
Blossoms and buds, by Bobbie Banford.
Diameter 7.5 cm $425

2 Pink Flower Bouquet
by Bobbie Banford.
Diameter 7.5 cm $485

3 Bouquet of Pansies
Diamond cut on the base, by Bob Banford.
Diameter 8.2 cm $1280

4 Multi-Flower Star Bouquet
Cut garland on top and star cut on the base, magnum weight. Single piece by Bob Banford.
Diameter 9.3 cm $2650

5 Red Dahlia with Torsade
Transparent blue ground, cut with several small windows, star cut on the base, by Bob Banford.
Diameter: 7.5 cm $1280

6 Daisy with Buds
Diamond cut on the base, by Bob Banford.
Diameter 7.5 cm $640

7 Rose Branch
Two roses and three buds, window cut, diamond cut on the base, by Ray Banford.
Diameter 7.5 cm $700

8 Iris Bouquet
Opaque white ground, by Ray Banford.
Diameter 8.5 cm $885

9 Alpine Orchid
Blue bouquet, star cut on the
base, by Bob Banford.
Diameter 7.5 cm $790

10 Iris Basket
Green and white double overlay
with decorative cut, by Ray
Banford.
Diameter 8.0 cm $1800

11 Iris Bouquet
Diamnod cut on the base,
magnum weight by Ray
Banford.
Diameter 9.3 cm $885

12 Pansy
on filigree with blue and white
torsade, by Bob Banford.
Diameter 7.5 cm $975

13 Blue Dahlias
Red and white double overlay,
by Bob Banford.
Diameter 7.5 cm $1100

14 Pansy
on filigree with white torsade,
by Bob Banford.
Diameter 7.5 cm $975

15 Iris Basket
Yellow and white double
overlay with decorative cut, by
Ray Banford.
Diameter 7.5 cm $1890

Lampwork technique.

Signature: millefiori cane with
white and black "B" (Ray),
white with blue rim and black
"B" (Bob), white with zigzag
blue rim and blue "B" (Bobbie).

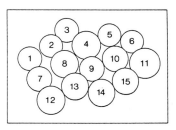

Roland (Rick) Ayotte

Paperweights by the American paperweight artist Rick Ayotte

Red-brown Admiral
and blue

Pyrrhopyge Creon Butterfly
with flowered twigs. Clear ground. 50 made. See bird paperweights for manufacturing technique and signature. Diameter 9 cm $915

Roland (Rick) Ayotte

Birds and Flowered Twigs

1 Magpie
with wild rhododendron blossoms. $725

2 Wood Thrush
with blue flax blossoms. White opaque ground. 50 made. $790

3 Magpie
with wild rhododendron blossoms. Miniature size. $300

4 Blue Titmice
with berry twig. White opaque ground. 75 made. $670

5 Magpie
with wild rhododendron blossoms. White opaque ground. $820

6 Scarlet Tanager
with tulip-tree blossoms. 75 made. $820

7 Birch Siskin
with palm branch. White
opaque ground. 50 made. $725

8 Hermit Thrush
with violets. 75 made. $790

9 Golden-Front Leaf Bird
with orchids. 75 made. $915

10 Cardinal
with white flowers. Miniature
size. $300

11 Scarlet Tanager
with tulip-tree blossoms.
Miniature size. $300

12 Oriole
with three young in the nest in a
pear tree. Blue ground. 50
made. $975

Lampwork technique.

Quantity made: 25, 50 or 75.
Signature hand-engraved on the
rim: "Ayotte", serial number,
quantity made and year, for
example 15/50 '91.
Diameter ca. 9-10 cm Miniature
weights ca. 5 cm
$725-915, miniatures ca. $300

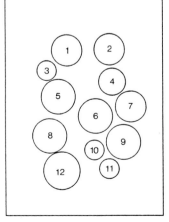

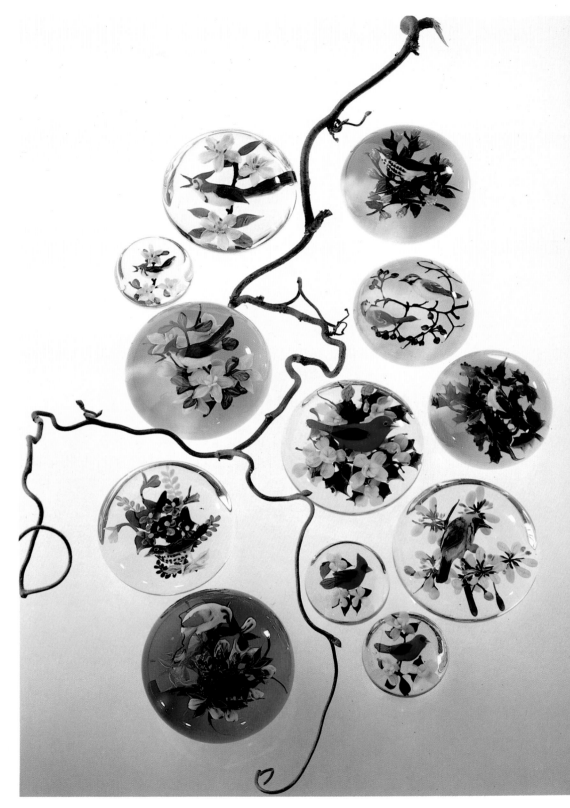

Roland (Rick) Ayotte

Fruit and Flower Paperweights.

1 Rosa Indica
Delicate pink tea-rose bouquet with bluish-green leaves on a clear ground. 50 made.
Diameter 9.5 cm

2 Hungarian Rhapsody
Red poppy blossoms with blue and white flowers, clear background. 50 made, 1991 and 1992.
Diameter 9.5 cm

3 Damascene Plums
Three blue plums with white blossoms and green leaves, clear ground. 50 made, 1990 and 1991.
Diameter 9.5 cm

4 Crab apples
Arrangement of red and green apples with white apple blossoms and green leaves. 50 made, 1991 and 1992.
Diameter 9.5 cm

5 Dahlia
Large red individual blossom with two buds on a clear ground. Single piece, 1992.
Diameter 9 cm

6 Cosmos
Yellow and pink flowers with blue panicles, clear ground. Single piece, 1992.
Diameter 9 cm

1-6:
Lampwork technique.
Signature hand-engraved on the rim: "Ayotte", number made and year, for example AP/1 '92.
$915-1220

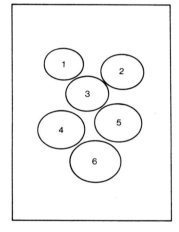

Chris Buzzini

1988

Flower paperweights with clear ground

Lampwork technique. Signature: "Buzzini" hand-engraved on the rim, usually plus year, abbreviated name, serial number and quantity. White cane with green center, "Buzzini" and year in blue. Quantities made: 25, 40 or 75.
Diameter 8 cm $455-915

1
2
3
4
5
6

Chris Buzzini

Two of the artist's paper-weights, made in various studios.

Illustrated below:
1 Butterfly with Pink Flower
on a light iridescent ground. Diameter 7.1 cm; 250 made. Signature: hand-engraved "Buzzini 41315" on base. Lundberg Studio, 1980.

This paperweight from the Correia Studio is almost identical:

2 Butterfly with Three Pink Flowers
on a bright iridescent ground. Diameter 7.3 cm; 100 made. Signature: hand-engraved "Correiä, 1983. Chris Buzzini worked at Correia Art Glass from 1982 to 1986. Limited edition LBCL 1.100.

1 and 2: $300

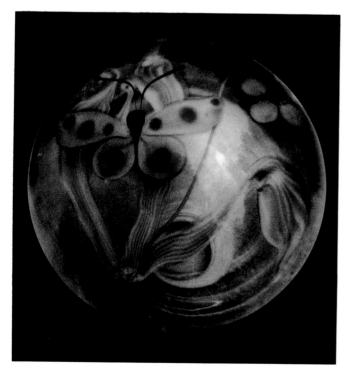

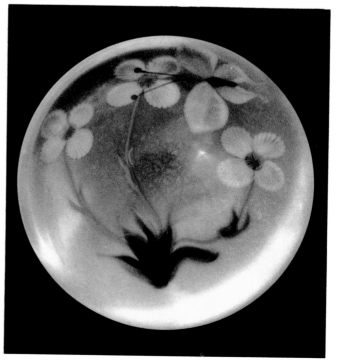

Jim Donofrio

1991 and 1992

1 Desert Flowers
Still life with cactus on sandy bottom.
Diameter ca. 8.5 cm $1035

2 Blue Crab
with shellfish on sandy bottom.
Diameter ca. 8.5 cm $820

3 Frog
with pine twig on sandy bottom.
Diameter ca. 8.5 cm $820

4 New Mexico
Still life in the desert, sandy bottom.
Diameter ca. 8.5 cm $1035

Lampwork technique. Signature engraved on lower rim: "Jim Donofrio", year and registry number.

1

3

4

2

Randall Grubb, Ken Rosenfeld, Gordon Smith & Chris Buzzini

post-1988

Flower Paperweights
Signatures
Randall Grubb:
Cane with black "G" on a white ground, also engraved on rim "Randall Grubb" and year.
Ken Rosenfeld:
Cane with blue "R" on a white ground, also engraved on rim "Ken Rosenfeld" and year.
Gordon Smith:
Engraved on rim "GES" and year.
Chris Buzzini:
Cane with blue letters and numbers, "Buzzini" and year. Also engraved on rim "Buzzini", year, registry letters, serial number and quantity made, for example, PP 12/25. Lampwork technique.

1 Blossom Bouquet
Stylized flowers on a clear ground. Single piece by Ken Rosenfeld.
Diameter 8.8 cm $550

2 Plum Blossoms
A twig with many small mallow-colored blossoms and buds, clear ground. Limited edition by Randall Grubb.
Diameter 7.9 cm $485

3 Lady-slipper
White orchid on a clear ground. Limited edition by Gordon Smith.
Diameter 7.6 cm $550

4 Pink Bouquet
with lilac flower panicles on a clear ground. Limited edition by Randall Grubb.
Diameter 7.6 cm $485

5 Red Lady-slipper
Orchid with green leaves on a clear ground. Limited edition by Gordon Smith.
Diameter 7.5 cm $550

6 Bellflowers
Pale pink flowers, green leaves and tendrils on a transparent blue ground. Limited edition by Gordon Smith.
Diameter 7.6 cm $610

7 Flower Bouquet
Stylized flowers over a white opaque ground, arranged in a bouquet. Single piece by Ken Rosenfeld.
Diameter 8.8 cm $610

8 Lilac Bouquet
with yellow flower panicles on a clear ground. Limited edition by Randall Grubb.
Diameter 7.6 cm $485

9 Cactus Garden
Various types of blooming cactus on a clear ground. Limited edition by Ken Rosenfeld.
Diameter 8.7 cm $670

10 Pink Orchid with Buds
Clear ground. Limited edition by Gordon Smith.
Diameter 7.7 cm $670

11 Bird-of-Paradise Flower
Strelitzia on a dark green ground. Limited edition by Gordon Smith.
Diameter 7.6 cm $550

12 Red Lady-Slipper
Orchid with green leaves on a transparent blue ground. Limited edition by Gordon Smith.
Diameter 7.5 cm $550

13 Grapes
Naturalistically portrayed grapevine with three bunches of dark blue grapes and green leaves, clear ground. Limited edition by Randall Grubb.
Diameter 7.6 cm $485

14 Thistles
Three orange thistle blossoms with pointed leaves on a clear ground. Limited edition by Randall Grubb.
Diameter 8.2 cm $725

15 California Flower
Orange California wildflowers with buds, green leaves and roots. By Chris Buzzini, 40 made.
Diameter 8.0 cm $485

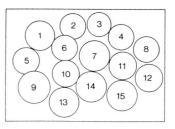

Ken Rosenfeld

1 Rose Bouquet
Three roses in different shades
of red with buds and green
leaves on a clear ground. One of
Ken Rosenfeld's first lampwork
motifs from his own studio.
Signed: "Ken Rosenfeld 1984";
white cane with a black "R".
Diameter 7.8 cm $485

2 Cabbage Rose
One red rose surrounded by
small blue and white stylized
flowers. Clear ground. Ken
Rosenfeld calls this motif
"American Liberty Bouquet".
Signature: white cane with
black "R" and hand-engraved
"Ken Rosenfeld 1987" on the
rim.
Diameter 7.8 cm $485

1

2

Randall Grubb

Grapes
Three realistically portrayed
bunches of green grapes on a
vine with green leaves. This
motif is on two levels (com-
pound) and was made by
lampwork.
Signature: white cane with
black "G" and hand-engraved
"Randall Grubb 1991" on the
rim.
Diameter 7.6 cm $485

▷

Charles Kaziun

1975-1985

1 Glitter-Heart
with millefiori canes, red and
green, and a blue and red
torsade on a white opaque
ground.
Diameter 5.2 cm

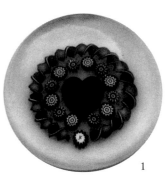

1

2

**2 Millefiori with Silhouette
Canes**
Fish, rabbit, turtle, cloverleaf,
goose and heart, one Clichy
rose and one cane with "K"
signature on a gold tinsel
ground.

3 Sunbonnet Sue
Silhouette paperweight. The
black and white silhouette of a
girl is surrounded by a two-
colored torsade, plus millefiori
canes with hearts, yellow
ground. Signature cane with
"K".

4 Morning Glory with Bud
on a white trellis with a yellow
ground. A small bee—made of
14-karat gold foil—sits in the
opened blossom.
Diameter 6 cm

5 Blue Clematis
with bud, yellow stamens,
mallow-colored opaque ground,
small gold bee on a green leaf.
Diameter 6 cm

6 Pansy
on a red opaque ground with a
small bee made of 14-karat gold
foil on a green leaf.
Diameter 5.8 cm

Many paperweights by Charles
Kazium have a "K" made of 14-
karat gold foil melted into the
underside.

1-6 $610-1825

3

Nontas and James Kontes

1984

**Strawberries on
White Filigree**
Two red berries, one unripe
green berry, and a white
blossom on sections of white
glass filament, dark green
transparent ground.

Signature: white cane with
twelve yellow star canes around
it, and a black "K" (James
Kontes).
Diameter 7.8 cm

Values: These paperweights
could not be purchased from the
Kontes brothers. They are both
trained glassmakers, at home
with the intricacies and
techniques of making glass
laboratory articles and scientific
apparatus. They make paperweights only in their spare time,
for their own pleasure. Their
paperweights—except for the
strawberries by James Kontes—
are very stylized portrayals of
flowers, fruit and snakes.
These few individual pieces
were given to good friends or
contributed to charity auctions
for worthy causes.

6

4

5

Johne Parsley
1989

Flower paperweights made by the trained American glassmaker Johne Parsley. Until about 1987 J. P. made only miniature paperweights no larger than 5.5 cm in diameter.

1 Spring Flowers
Transparent blue ground.

2 Pink Roses
Transparent cobalt blue ground, window cut.

3 Wildflower Bouquet with Pansies
Transparent blue ground.

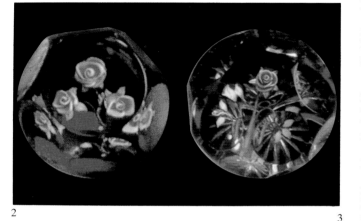

2

3

1

4 + 5

4 Pansies
Clear ground.

5 Wildflowers with Buds
and flower panicles. Clear ground.

Signature: Cane with blue "P" on a white ground, blue overlaid, also hand-engraved "JP" and year on the lower rim.
Diameter 5 to 6.5 cm
$610-915

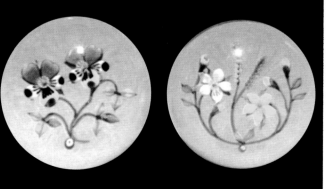

Paul Stankard

Flower Paperweights

1 Wood Violets
Lilac and white violets, clear ground. Signed 20.75 B127 1978 and "S" cane.

2 Wildflower
Orange blooming lily plant with "Root People", clear ground. Signed: Paul J. Stankard a72 1989.
Diameter 8.5 cm

3 Spider Orchid
Brassia caudata plant with roots on a clear ground. Signed 72/5 A84 1980 and "S" cane.
Diameter 8.0 cm

4 Blackberries
Berries and blossoms. Cloistered Botanical with "Root People". Signed: Paul J. Stankard D32 1989.
Height 13 cm

5 White Gentian
With "Root People" and clear ground. Signed: Paul J. Stankard A9 1990.
Diameter 7.8 cm

6 Blue Gentian
Open and still-closed gentian blossoms. Environmental with "Root People" and gold enclosures on a clear ground. Signed "P. Stankard 1988".

7 Forget-me-not
Blue forget-me-not on a clear ground. Signed: 1981 and "S" cane.
Diameter 7.6 cm

8 Blue Bottle Gentian
Blue closed gentian blossoms. Signed: Experimental B33 1980 and "S" cane.
Diameter 9.3 cm

9 Wildflower
Yellow blossoming lily plant with roots. Signed: Paul J. Stankard A77 1989.
Diameter 7.9 cm

10 Wild Pansy
on amethyst-colored ground. Signed: A068 1978 and "S" cane.
Diameter 7.2 cm

11 White Flax Blossom
with buds on a green ground. Signed: 20377 1980 and "S" cane.
Diameter 7.6 cm

**12 Pink Gentian
on stony ground**
Environmental with roots, orbs and "Root People". Signed: Paul J. Stankard A8 1990.
Diameter 7.8 cm

13 Meadowreath
Two yellow blossoms and panicles. Signed: Stankard 05375 1977.
Diameter 7.1 cm

14 Spiderwort Flower
Two blue blossoms and three little buds on a clear ground. Signed: 1975 and "PS" cane.
Diameter 7.1 cm

Lampwork technique.

1-3, 5-14: $1825-3660

4: $7310

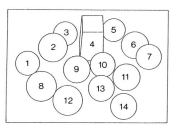

Paul J. Stankard
1990-1992

1-4 Spring Beauty Botanical Sculptures
Every Botanical is a unique single piece. The signature of Paul J. Stankard, registry number and year are hand-engraved at the back of the lower rim.
Height 13 to 15 cm
$6100-15,245

Opposite page, below:
5-6 Environmentals with "Root People"
White daisies, blue forget-me-not, pink wild roses, red raspberries, bees, roots with "Orbs" and "Root People".
Diameter 8.5 cm $2745

2–4 ▷

"Roots, Root People and Orbs- a new Mythology, I call them spirits under the Earth."
Paul Joseph Stankard

1   5 + 6 ▷

Delmo and Debbie Tarsitano

Flower paperweights by the American paperweight artists Delmo Tarsitano (#3 and 9) and Debbie Tarsitano, made by lampwork technique. All the examples have a "DT" millefiori cane and are single pieces.

1 Bouquet with Berries
Panicles and blossoms, window cut.
Diameter 8.5 cm $1525

2 Wild Rose with Hip
Diameter 8.5 cm $1490

3 Strawberries
with pink blossoms on a moss-green ground.
Diameter 8.0 cm $1128

4 Blossoming Lucky Clover
Strawberry cut on the base.
Diameter 8.7 cm $1065

5 Debbie's Mother's-Day Flowers
Window cut, star cut on the base.
Diameter 8.6 cm $1065

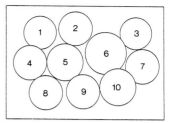

6 English Garden
Summer garden with red and
yellow mallows (hollyhocks).
Diameter 9.5 cm $3965

7 Violet Bouquet
on pale lilac ground, 15 window
cuts.
Diameter 8.0 cm $855

8 Flower Arrangement
Red and blue blossoms with
buds, star cut on the base.
Diameter 8.0 cm $1400

9 Strawberry with Blossoms
Star cut on the base.
Diameter 7.7 cm $1130

10 Wild Rose Branch
with bud and hip. Window cut,
star cut on the base.
Diameter 8.6 cm $1340

Delmo Tarsitano

1988

Action Salamander
With roots, stones and grass.
Magnum paperweight from the
Earth Life Series by Delmo
Tarsitano, USA, single piece.
Lampwork technique. Signa-
ture: millefiori cane with "DT".
Diameter 10.5 cm $2745

Delmo Tarsitano

1988

Earth Life Series
Insects and reptiles amid roots, flowers and grasses.

Lampwork technique. Signature: millefiori cane with "DT". Single pieces.

1 Earth Life
Wasp with strawberries and blossoms.
Diameter 9.0 cm $1800

2 Earth Life
Wasp and two spiders in webs, green ground.
Diameter 9.0 cm $1800

3 Earth Life
Green adder with roots, grasses and blossoms.
Diameter 8.7 cm $1815

4 Earth Life
Spider in a web.
Diameter 8 cm $1585

5 Earth Life
White snake with beetle.
Diameter 7.5 cm $1160

6 Earth Life
Red salamander with roots and grasses.
Diameter 9.0 cm $1770

7 Earth Life
Spider in a web and blue bindweed.
Diameter 8.8 cm $1615

8 Earth Life
Brown sand adder with white flower.
Diameter 7.8 cm $1340

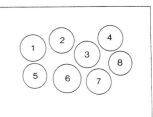

Victor Trabucco and his sons David and Jon Trabucco

1992

Paperweights with flowers and berries on a clear ground, made by lampwork.

1-2 Victor Trabucco
Pansies and buttercups, strawberries with white blossoms, pink camellia and seed pod, pink camellia and red raspberries.
Diameter 10 cm, magnum weight. $1100-1340

3-4 Victor Trabucco
Twig with red berries and acorns. Bouquet with pink blossoms and blue berries.
Diameter 8 cm $550-610

5-7 David and Jon Trabucco
Blue anemone with bud. Red raspberries and white blossoms. Silkflowers in white, blue, red, violet and pink.
Signature: green cane with black "T". $300-400

1

2

7

3

4

5

6

Victor, David and Jon Trabucco

Flower paperweights made by the American paperweight artist Victor Trabucco and his sons David and Jon Trabucco.

1 Lady-slipper Orchid
Blue ground.
Diameter 8 cm $665

2 Twig with Red Fruit and White Blossoms
Clear ground.
Diameter 8 cm $600

3 Silk Rose "Prunice"
Blue ground.
Diameter 8 cm $665

4 Yellow Morning Glory
Blue ground.
Diameter 8 cm $600

5 Violet Rose "Cardinal de Richelieu"
Clear ground, window cut.
Diameter 8 cm $700

6 Magnum "Golden Wings", two yellow roses
Light blue opaque ground.
Diameter 10 cm $1270

7 Magnum Bouquet with Pink Rose "Celeste"
Blue ground.
Diameter 10 cm $1270

8 Magnum "Cattleya Orchids"
Blue ground.
Diameter 10 cm $1370

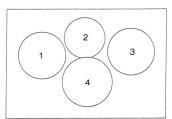

9 Bouquet with Pink Rose "Celeste"
Blue ground.
Diameter 8 cm $785

10 Red Rose "Prince Noir"
Blue ground.
Diameter 8 cm $665

11 Yellow Rose "Golden Wings"
Light blue opaque ground.
Diameter 8 cm $665

12 Violet Rose "Cardinal de Richelieu"
Clear ground.
Diameter 8 cm $665

13 "Winter" Bouquet with White Rose
David and Jon.
Diameter 7.5 cm $395

14 "Summer" Bouquet with Blue Clematis
David and Jon.
Diameter 7.5 cm $395

15 "Autumn" Bouquet with Pink Dahlia
David and Jon.
Diameter 7.5 cm $395

16 "Spring" Bouquet with Pink Anemones
David and Jon.
Diameter 7.5 cm $395

Lampwork technique. Signature: green cane with black letters "VT" or "T", sometimes only hand-engraved "Trabucco" and year (for example, with a colored ground).

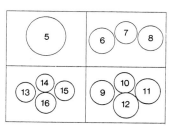

Mayauel Ward

1990-1992

*Flower arrangements made by
lampwork on clear or black
grounds, and his "Desert
Flowers" on sandy ground.*

1 Desert Flowers
Red blossoms and buds on
sandy ground, bent branch.
Diameter ca. 6 cm $395

2 Cattleya
Lilac orchids on a black ground.
Diameter ca. 6 cm $355

3 Desert Flowers
White blossoms and buds on
sandy ground, dried branch.
Diameter ca. 6 cm $380

4 Bouquet
Three red trumpet flowers,
yellow twig with blossoms, two
panicles and orchid leaves.
Diameter ca. 6 cm

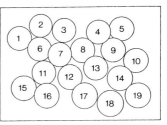

5 Lady-slipper
Lilac orchid with roots on a
black ground.
Diameter ca. 6 cm $355

6 Bouquet
White, light blue and mallow-
colored flowers on a black
ground.
Diameter ca. 6 cm $395

7 Desert Flowers
Yellow and mallow-colored
blossoms amid stones on a
sandy ground.
Diameter ca. 6 cm $395

8 Asters
on a black ground.
Diameter ca. 6 cm $290

9 Flower Arrangement
Yellow and mallow-colored
blossoms on a black ground.
Diameter ca. 6 cm $395

10 Desert Flowers
Light blue asters and buds on a
sandy ground.
Diameter ca. 6 cm $380

11 Evergreen
Blue flowers, black ground.
Diameter ca. 6 cm $230

12 Twig of Flowers
with red blossoms and buds on
a black ground.
Diameter 6 cm $355

13 Desert Flowers
Light blue blossoms, greenish-
brown leaves and dried
branches on a sandy ground.
Diameter 6 cm $380

14 Lady-slipper
Pink orchid with roots, clear
ground.
Diameter 6 cm $170

15 Summer Flowers
Arrangement of white, yellow,
mallow-colored and blue
flowers on a clear ground.
Diameter 6 cm $380

16 Desert Flowers
Yellow blossoms and buds
amid stones on a sandy ground.
Diameter 6 cm $395

17 Peach-colored Dahlia
on a black ground.
Diameter 6 cm $290

18 Red Trumpet Flower
Twig with blossoms and buds
on a black ground.
Diameter 6 cm $355

19 Desert Flowers
White, red, mallow-colored and
light blue flowers amid stones
on a sandy ground.
Diameter 6 cm $395

Rose Paperweights by Various Factories and Artists

*All examples, with the
exception of the antique Clichy
'Flower on White Filigree' (#8)
made since 1978.*

1 Yellow Roses with Bud
on iridescent ground. Sillars,
Orient & Flume, 250 made.
Diameter 8.2 cm $300

2 Pink Wild Roses
on a light blue opaque ground.
Paul Stankard, 1978, single
piece.
Diameter 7 cm $3000

3 Rosa Indica
Rose bouquet on a clear ground.
Rick Ayotte, 50 made.
Diameter 9.6 cm $975

4 Yellow Clichy Roses
on a blue ground. Saint-Louis,
1976, 400 made.
Diameter 8 cm $855

**5 Upright Pink Rose with
Leaves and Buds**
Sillars, Orient & Flume, 250
made.
Diameter 8.1 cm $490

6 White Lady
White roses with buds on a
glowing blue ground, window
cut. Saint-Louis, 1991, 250
made.
Diameter 8.2 cm $975

7 Silk Rose "Prunice"
on a clear ground. Victor
Trabucco, 1991, limited edition.
Diameter 8.3 cm $610

8 Flower on White Filigree
with a wreath of millefiori
canes and six pink Clichy roses.
Clichy, mid-19th century, single
piece.
Diameter 7.2 cm $7310

9 Yellow Peace Rose
Upright yellow rose. Daniel
Salazar, Lundberg Studio, 250
made.
Diameter 5.8 cm $365

10 Red Rose with Bud
on a transparent blue ground,
small window cut, star cut on
base. Johne Parsley, 1986,
single piece.
Diameter 6.1 cm $915

11 Red Rose "Prince Noir"
on a clear ground, window cut.
Victor Trabucco, 1991, limited
edition.
Diameter 8 cm $610

12 Pink Roses and Beetle
on a green ground. Baccarat,
1985, 200 made.
Diameter 7.8 cm $790

**13 Wild Rose Twig with
Blossom and Hip**
Debbie Tarsitano, 1986, single
piece.
Diameter 8.5 cm $1525

14 Julia's Rose
Upright pink rose. Daniel
Salazar, Lundberg Studio, 250
made.
Diameter 5.8 cm $365

15 Rose Twig
Two roses and three buds,
window cut, diamond cut on
base. Ray Banford, limited
edition.
Diameter 7.5 cm $725

16 Rosa Indica
Miniature rose, window cut.
Rick Ayotte, 1991, single piece.
Diameter 5.2 cm $240

Illustrations on page 166.

**Rose Paperweights
from Various
Factories and
Artists**

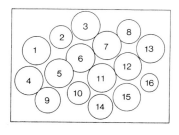

Index of Makers

A.L.T. 25
Abelman Art Studio 21, 39
Alexander, 141
Antoniwald 22
Ayotte, Roland (Rick) 16, 43, 44, 146, 148, 165

Baccarat 13, 14, 16, 18, 23, 26, 27-30, 35, 36, 43, 57, 58, 63, 66-73, 78, 79, 94-96, 165
Bacchus & Sons 32, 82
Bacchus of Birmingham 13
Banford, Bob 43, 49, 144, 145
Banford, Bobbie 43, 144
Banford, Ray 43, 144, 145, 165
Beyer 142
Bigaglia, Pietor 11, 12, 25, 66
Bussolin, Domenico 25
Buzzini, Christopher (Chris) 39, 43, 46, 50, 135, 149, 150, 151

Caithness Glass Ltd. 16, 30-35, 120, 130, 134
Cambridge Glass 36
Cape Cod Glass Co. 36
China 35, 91, 93
Clichy 13, 14, 23, 27-30, 32, 36, 54, 57, 63, 66-69, 72, 74, 75, 142, 165
Compagnie des Cristalleries de Baccarat 26
Compagnie des Cristalleries de Saint-Louis 29, 108, 112
Correia Art Glass 21, 39, 46, 135, 136, 149
Correia, Steven 39
Cristallerie de Sèvres et Clichy 28

Deacons, John 35, 121
Donofrio, Jim 43, 46, 150
Drysdale, Stuart 32

Erlacher, Max 52
Ferro & Lazzarini 25, 114
Franchini, Giovanni B. 25
Franklin Flint Glass Works 36

Gillinder and Son 36
Gillinder, William T. 36

Gooderham, John 47
Grubb, Randall (Randy) 43, 47, 150-152

Hacker, Harold 48
Hansen, Robert 48
Hansen, Ronald 48
Harrachsche, Hütte 22
Highland Paperweights 33
Holmes, Peter 34, 130, 132
Hopkins, John 36
Hutchison, Ron 34

"J" Jay Glass (also "Jay" Glass) 35, 122, 127
Jarves, Denning 36
Josephinenhütte 22

Kaziun, Charles 43, 48, 152, 153
Kaziun, Charles II 48
Kontes, James 49, 153
Kontes, Nontas 49, 153
Kunckel, Johann 11

Labrino, Dominick 49
Leighton, Thomas 36
Libbey, William 36
Loetz 21
Lotton Art Glass 40, 137
Lotton, Charles 40, 137
Lotton, Daniel 137
Lotton, David 40, 137
Lotton, John 40, 137
Lundberg Glass Studio 16, 21, 40, 46, 139, 138, 165
Lundberg, James 40
Lundberg, Steven 40, 138, 139
Lutz, Nicholas 36, 84

Manson, William 34, 124, 126
Moncrieff (Monart Glass) 33
Monot & Cie 29
Moretti & Fratelli 25
Mount Washington Glass Co. 36, 54, 82, 84

New England Glass Co. 86

Orient & Flume 21, 41, 46, 140, 141, 165
Owens, Michael 36

P.Y. Glass Co. 33
Pairpoint Glass 36
Pantin 29, 30, 54, 58, 63, 81
Parabelle Glass 42, 142
Parsley, Johne 43, 49, 154, 165
Pellat Jr., Apsley 13
Perthshire Glass 32, 58, 127
Pierre, François 36
Poore, Ed 52
Powell, J & Sons 30

Riedelsche, Hütte 22
Rosenfeld, Ken 39, 43, 50, 150-152

Saint-Louis 13, 14, 16, 18, 19, 23, 26, 28, 30, 36, 43, 59, 63,
66, 67, 69, 71, 72, 75, 76, 78, 84, 96, 97, 101, 102, 104, 106,
108, 165
Salazar, Daniel 40, 138, 165
Salazar, David 40, 143
Sandwich Glass 36, 84
Sautner, Barry 51
Scott, Alan 35
Scrutton, Doris 42
Scrutton, Gary 42
Selkirk Glass Ltd. 16, 34, 129, 130, 132
Sèvres 28
Simpson, Josh 42, 144
Smith, Gordon 43, 49, 50, 150, 151
Stankard, Paul 16, 43, 44, 46, 51, 54, 63, 154-156, 165
Strathearn Glass 32, 33, 128

Tarsitano, Debbie 43, 52, 158, 165
Tarstiano, Delmo 30, 43, 52, 158-160
Terris, Colin 34
Tiffany 21
Toso, Fratelli 25, 113, 114
Trabucco, David 43, 52, 161, 162
Trabucco, Jon 43, 52, 161, 162
Trabucco, Victor 30, 43, 52, 160, 162, 165

Vasart Glass 32, 33

Ward, Mayauel 39, 53, 164
Whitefriars 30, 31, 34, 115-119, 120
Whittemore, Francis 43, 53

Ysart, Antoine 33
Ysart, Pablo (Paul) Moreno 32, 33, 34, 57, 130, 134
Ysart, Salvador 33
Ysart, Vincent 33